Enjoy the Flow!

Wes

"I Got This"

Living in the Flow of
God's Kingdom Economy

Wesley K. Zinn

PRESS

"I Got This"
Living in the Flow of God's Kingdom Economy
by Wesley K. Zinn

Printed in the United States of America

ISBN 9781628719215

Cover design and artwork by Erik Johnson

www.xulonpress.com

Endorsements

The revealed word of God brings light. This was my experience reading Wesley Zinn's book "I Got This". It is a refreshing approach to giving and receiving. I found it both helpful and liberating in removing wrong attitudes and approaches to giving. This book is a must read for those who desire to become a greater conduit of blessing in the earth. It will help remove the sense of duty, and release us into the joy of giving. God loves a cheerful giver!

Jeff Collins
Jeff Collins Ministry

This is a magnificent book of transformational kingdom principles concerning the grace of giving, living in God's economy, and experiencing financial freedom. With clear Biblical teaching and insights that flow from a lifestyle of radical generosity, Pastor Wesley teaches on the heart attitude of worship that unlocks the flow of heaven. He provides us with a fresh perspective on giving as a spiritual act of worship that flows from our relationship with God.

Catherine Brown
Founder/Director, Gatekeepers Global Ministries

Asking Pastor Wes to speak at our annual leadership conference in Uganda was one of the best decisions I have ever made for the conference. His down to earth lifestyle, along with his integrity in leadership and God's resources has ministered to all of us. He opened our eyes to a generous God and released us from a God we always had to bribe if we stood any chance of getting blessed. The impact of his teaching at our leaders' network was so phenomenal that now his message is being echoed by many of our pastors to their congregations. I wish I could put a copy of this book in the hands of every African leader from church to government.

Bishop Arnold Muwonge
Founder, Nations Discipleship Enterprise
and Kampala Children's Centre

Acknowledgements

To Pam, who walks this journey of faith with me every day. You embody the truth and life I've attempted to capture in these pages. Your unfailing love, encouragement, and belief in me is one of my greatest treasures.

To Wellspring Church and Pastor Rick, who create the community and leadership for God's life-giving truth and presence. I'm inspired by your passionate desire to see the Lord's kingdom come and his will done on earth.

To my parents, who instilled the foundations of truth and life in me from the beginning. I'm grateful for the heritage you've stewarded and passed on to me.

To Nathan and Kyle, who made my life more meaningful than I would have thought. You are my pride and joy, and you still cause courage to rise up in me.

To Erik, who brightened this book with his creativity. I'm grateful for your skill and insightful perspective.

To Julia, Dawn, Mike, Erik, Peter, and Ed, who gave of themselves to help me make my thoughts readable. I appreciate all your encouragement and better yet every one of your critiques.

Table of Contents

Foreword

T he truths you will encounter in the pages of this book are living and active! They have been forged and tested in a life lived unto the Lord and in the service of his people. I have watched these truths give life and release blessing into others.

Through the centuries the church has definitely been confused and confusing in its attitude and message about money, finances, and wealth: vows of poverty, the economics of Christendom, a prosperity gospel, incessant fundraising by televangelists, marketplace ministry. How are Christ-followers to relate to money and finances in this world? What does it mean to give in and from the economy of the kingdom of God?

This book is not a theology of wealth and finance. It is a testimony and witness to the power of faith-filled obedience to the joy of generosity; to the capacity to receive and steward increase; to the ability to live in abundance without being consumed by mammon; to the faith to prophesy, proclaim, and declare truth that will change lives and life situations.

I have benefited from these testimonies. They have become a witness in my own life and circumstances and to the church that Wes and I have the privilege to serve together. Read this book with your heart and hands open — your heart open to receive blessing and your hands open to give the blessing away to others.

Rev. Rick McKinniss
Senior Leader, Wellspring Church

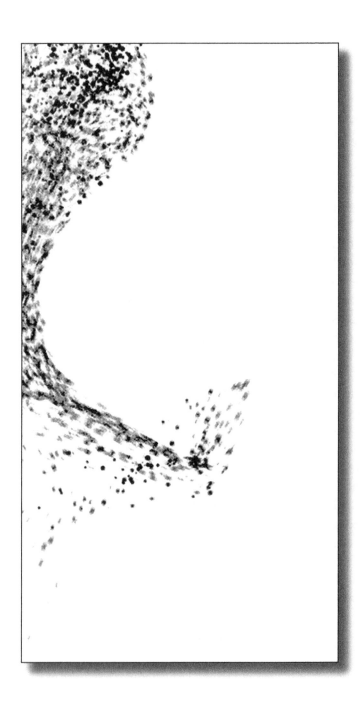

Introduction

"Where can I buy nine hundred bananas?" The request surprised and confused my hosts. Nine hundred pastors and church leaders gathered for the annual Rising Tide conference in the village of Wakiso on the outskirts of Kampala, Uganda. I was scheduled to speak the next day, and for my teaching illustration I would need nine hundred bananas.

The next morning on the way to the conference, my driver detoured our van into a bustling outdoor market. Patrons interacted with eager grocers, while the aroma of fresh produce competed with foul odors. Eagerly anticipating the adventure, I opened the van door. "No, you must stay here," came the firm instruction from my driver and his assistant. They knew that even the sight of a Mzungu (white person) would undermine all their bargaining power. So, the Mzungus obediently waited in the van until, finally, a whole group returned, all with armloads of bananas. They had fulfilled my request while making a few vendors very happy. On to the conference we drove with the tropical heat causing the smell of quickly ripening bananas to fill our nostrils. At the conclusion of my teaching that day, each attendee held a banana with which to remember the lesson—at least until they all ate their illustrations. What was the teaching about? Giving.

I had been invited specifically to speak about giving. The organizer of the conference had heard some of my teaching, and he requested that I share it with his network of pastors in Uganda. At first the thought unsettled me. I would be the "rich" American who came to a developing nation to teach poor and even impoverished people about money. How condescending! I didn't want to be that guy. I wanted to be the guy requested to speak about God's love, joy, and forgiveness. I wanted to be the guy people wanted to see after the message, not the guy they wanted to avoid.

To my surprise, I've become that guy—the guy people request to teach about giving. I've preached on giving in a number of countries and in many churches, even churches I barely know (and they barely know me.) I've rallied the troops as the keynote speaker for the giving campaigns of other churches and ministries. I've flown to developing nations to speak at conferences where all the attendees walked for miles, and sometimes days, just to get there. What fascinates me is that I've truly enjoyed it, and by and large so have the congregations and audiences! They must, or they wouldn't keep asking me back and spreading the word.

Why? What am I sharing that others not only find helpful but welcome and even desire? I'm sharing freedom. Through the teaching, people find a release of freedom instead of guilt. They find a release of joy instead of depression. Instead of a formula for figuring it out, I simply share from my experience of living it out. And my experience is one of freedom.

When we hear about freedom in the area of finances, we usually think that the best way—or maybe the only way—to find freedom is to become comfortably wealthy so that we no longer have to struggle to make ends meet. However, I'm referring to a much more significant freedom, where the concern and weightiness of finances is replaced with peace and joy without fear or concern, a freedom completely unrelated to any specific financial circumstances, a spiritual freedom we not only experience but in which we can actually abide.

I am currently a pastor of a very healthy church, but my path to this point has not been a straight line, and neither have my finances. In my earliest years, I was an MK (Missionary Kid), as my parents were full-time missionaries. We lived in a mud-walled house in a very primitive village. The standard of living was quite low, and let's just say, so were the finances. Later, I put myself through college by working every hour I could on a dairy farm because every additional hour was another four dollars! After graduation I entered the business world, where I was quite successful, reaching the executive level of a huge international corporation. Then I left it all behind to accept the invitation to join the pastoral staff of the church we were attending, the same church I am still pastoring. With that transition, I also left behind the majority of my salary and many of the benefits and perks associated with my position. (Of course, I traded them for other perks!)

I traveled plenty for my jobs in business, and I saw the world from that perspective. I've flown on corporate jets, I've been entertained on private yachts, and I've slept in lavish locations. But I've also always had a heart for missions, so I've viewed the world through those lenses as well. Along with being an MK, I've been on numerous missions trips and ministry travels. I've been called on to pray while standing in the center of one of the poorest, most destitute slums in the world. I've rolled up my sleeves and worked shoulder to shoulder with survivors in the aftermaths of natural disasters. I've danced with small gatherings of worshipers well into night's darkness in tribal villages. I have been extremely privileged to have such wide and varied experiences and views of the world. It's a grand world that only God could create, and it's also a fallen world that our sin has greatly stained.

I've seen a significant spectrum of circumstances and environments broader than I could imagine. That is on the outside, the naturally observable side. But God calls and equips us to see with spiritual eyes as well. To the discerning spirit, the atmospheres and spiritual climates have been equally disparate. I've also observed with glaring clarity that the two spectrums don't easily and automatically line up—not at all. For instance, I've attended corporate events that were seemingly filled and overflowing with abundance but were cloaked in dark, heavy-spirited atmospheres. I've witnessed multimillion-dollar guys making multimillion-dollar decisions filled with ulcer-creating fear (not just stress but genuine fear.) At other times I've witnessed joy unbounded flooding the penniless assemblies of the impoverished. On one occasion a classroom of church planters and leaders from the tribal Kuvi people group of eastern India sat before me as I taught them in the basics of the Bible. Repeatedly, and nearly without warning, a student would break out in a worship song, causing the others to hurriedly fumble through their songbooks so they could join in the chorus. Those who didn't have songbooks joined the rhythm section, bringing intricate drumbeats to an inspiring crescendo. The songbooks were tattered but treasured notebooks in which they had hand-copied every new song they had heard, and the drums were the sophisticated sounds of their hands pounding the desks in front of them. Each time this happened I stood humbled. I was unable to join in their Kuvi language praise and equally inadequate to take part in the sophisticated rhythms, but joy welled up in my spirit all the same.

How can overflowing abundance and fear coexist? Why did joy spring forth from impoverished people? Natural and simple observations are clearly inadequate to even describe, let alone understand, the different environments and circumstances and how the spiritual climate and the human spirit can, despite those circumstances, create such disparate responses. We need to see in the natural *and* in the spiritual. We need to discern deeper perspectives and understanding.

The differences in circumstances of those around us, let alone those around the world, can be nearly incomparable. There is also the undeniable reality of the ever-present needy around us. As Christians, I believe we all have a responsibility to seek and work toward equality and actively help those in need. Yet, our charge as Christians also is to have eyes to see and ears to hear. We observe and serve in the natural, and we also know in our spirit and our understanding that improving circumstances alone does not bring the full transformation offered to everyone though the power and presence of Jesus, our Savior and the one who sets us free.

We are to observe, and we are to discern. There are many wonderful books, teachings, and tools to aid us in better management and even stewardship of our resources. But there is a significant difference between good management of what we have and spiritual freedom in the realm of finances. To that end, it is my desire to share with you from my own experiences, my lifelong faith, my ever deepening relationship with God, my years of studying the Scriptures, my observations from many perspectives, and from what I believe God has placed in my heart and in my understanding. It is my desire that through what I share you will come to experience complete spiritual freedom in the area of finances.

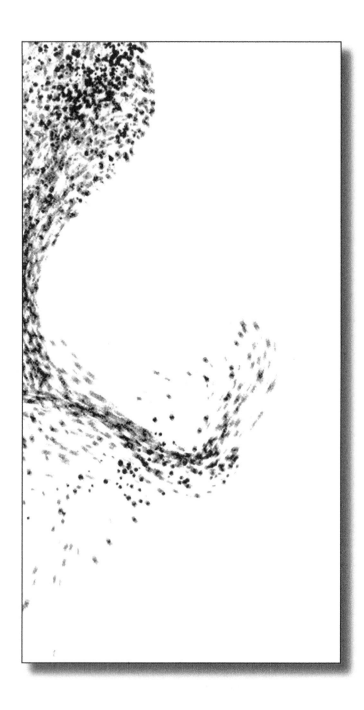

Freedom in Finances

It is for freedom that Christ has set us free. Stand firm, then, and do not let yourselves be burdened again by a yoke of slavery. (Galatians 5:1)

I felt a bit awkward standing in the first-grade lunch line until my son Nathan smiled up at me. He shared a young boy's joy and pride of knowing his father was there beside him. When my sons were in preschool, I began the practice of spending one day each year experiencing their school day. The teachers didn't know what to do with me, but my sons and I enjoyed it. On this particular day, after a morning of sitting in chairs that made me appear much taller than I am, reading stories to the class, and helping with math assignments, I made my way with the students to the corridor outside the school cafeteria. Once we had all taken our designated places neatly lined up against the side of the hall, the teacher handed off responsibility to the cafeteria crew and quickly disappeared for her midday break. That's when I noticed Eric, one of Nathan's friends, and the tears silently rolling down his cheeks.

"Eric, what's wrong?" I quickly asked.

"I forgot my drink in the classroom." Eric had brought his lunch to school, but in the rush to fall into ranks with his classmates to make their lunch-hour trek, he left his drink behind.

"That's okay, Eric. Just run back to the classroom and grab it," I said.

"I can't. We're not allowed to leave the lunch line."

I tried to reassure him. "It'll be okay, Eric. I'm sure they'll give you a drink in the cafeteria." My adult perspective still did not appreciate the enormity of his crisis.

"But I don't have any money," he sobbed.

"Oh, Eric, buddy, don't worry. I've got money. I'll buy you a drink."

Breakthrough! In a moment Eric's countenance changed. Life was going to be okay. In fact, wiping the tears from his cheeks, Eric asked boldly, "Could I get a Sunny Delight?"

What a poignant illustration that is of our relationship with our heavenly Father. All too often we feel as helpless and hopeless as Eric felt. From our perspective, there simply is no solution to the predicament we're in. We don't have what we need, and we sure don't have the means to acquire it. We are as trapped as a boy in a lunch line. The constraints and bindings may be invisible, but they are oh so real.

One of the names of God in the Bible is Jehovah-Jireh, meaning "the Lord provides." Yet, from our limited perspective, we are clearly out of provision, and there is no conceivable way the situation can change. We simply must endure a struggling life, settling for less than what we want, even less than what we need. We believe a life of lack is our destiny. We live constrained and bound by our limitations, all the while standing in the presence of Jehovah-Jireh. The fact is, our limits do not limit him. If we receive him, our limits shouldn't limit us either. We shouldn't view our lives as always settling for lack and less than.

The exclamation point of my exchange with young Eric was when he asked, "Could I get a Sunny Delight?" In the previous moment, Eric's circumstances paralyzed him. Even as I talked him through the various options, all he saw were dead ends. However, the moment his perspective shifted off his circumstances and onto me, a new reality presented itself. The facts remained the same: He'd forgotten his drink, he was not allowed to return to his classroom, and he had no money. However, a provider who was neither restricted nor limited by circumstances changed everything, a provider so wonderful, so capable, so caring and compassionate that Eric, without hesitation, didn't settle for water or even milk. No, he went for it. He asked for a Sunny Delight!

I wasn't even sure what a Sunny Delight was. I supposed it was some bottled specialty drink, but without hesitance I said, "Of course, buddy." It wasn't a calculated, justified decision. I didn't evaluate the young boy's studiousness, proper behavior, and worthiness throughout the morning. I didn't compare him to the other students to determine if I would grant this favor. My immediate response was to grant Eric the desire of his request. A Sunny Delight? Sure! It was simply a compassionate response. In fact, it was my delight to delight him with a Sunny Delight!

You might think this is a sweet story, but it does not actually portray the real-world challenges we all face every day: real bills, real facts about our income and the limits of our bank accounts, real frustrations from the unexpected doctors' bills, car repairs, home repairs, our son's braces, or our mother's new wheelchair. The specifics may vary, but the picture remains quite consistent. Real life sabotages our financial peace of mind. For many of us there never seems to be quite enough money to go around. If we could just have a little bit more, if there were a few less of the unexpected withdrawals on our bank account, we would be satisfied. We're not asking to be independently wealthy (although that would be wonderful); we just want a little bit more, a little more cushion, a little more breathing room. We're confident a little more would relieve stress, lift burdens, and give us a lot more freedom.

Freedom in Finances

"It is for freedom that Christ has set us free" (Galatians 5:1). As believers in Christ, we raise this verse like a grand banner over our lives, but how many of us really believe it? Along with salvation, do we believe Christ's purpose and redeeming work was to allow us to live in the fullness of liberty? And why do we find it most difficult to experience this freedom when it comes to finances, even if we embrace the declaration of this verse for most other aspects of our lives? Even if we don't live in the fullness of the declaration, we can embrace the ideal of the vision nonetheless. We can truly believe Christ desires for us to live in freedom. Yet when it comes to the realm of finances, the thought

of applying this great statement of our faith and embracing the heart of our God seems incongruous. Why is that?

Finances are as real as any other area of our lives, and they impact our Christian walk as much as any other area. They cause us to work, consuming much of our time and energy. Finances demand our attention, impact our priorities, shape our perspectives, dictate many of our choices, and influence nearly every aspect of our lives. We will uproot ourselves and our families in order to get a job or improve our income. What we do, where we go, what we purchase, and how we live all require a financial assessment. And every one of these decisions, choices, and commitments can tire us out, induce stress, cause relationship tensions, and even shape our understanding of ourselves and of God.

So why do we find it hard to believe that Christ truly desires to set us free in the area of finances? Why is it difficult to embrace God's heart for us to live free from financial stress when it is for freedom that Christ has set us free? The New Living Translation renders Galatians 5:1 this way: *"So Christ has really set you free. Make sure that you stay free."* The reality is, if we do not feel we are set free in our finances, we will not even feel the opportunity to live free, and we surely will not stay free.

Struggling to Make Sense of It All

How do we reconcile this declaration of Scripture with the reality of our lives? How do we understand God's heart for us to live in freedom in all areas in view of the reality of our personal circumstances? Where's the disconnect? Are we interpreting God's Word correctly? Do we have the right attitude about the circumstances in which we find ourselves in this world? We all face the clash between scriptural promises and our financial challenges. We try to reconcile this conflict and make sense of our situations while still believing in a powerful God and the many Bible passages about money. We end up defaulting to any number of conclusions in our attempt to make sense of it all. Many of these are poorly drawn conclusions that aren't accurate. They don't reflect the Father's heart, and they don't set us free. Even a quick review of some of our conclusions reveals how unsatisfying they are. Do any of these sound familiar?

The punitive conclusion. God is punishing me for either not handling my finances correctly or not living my life holy enough. I must be doing something wrong. Maybe God doesn't even care about me. I must become a better Christian so God will be happy with me. I will never have God's blessings until I earn his approval. Until then, I am simply failing in my Christian walk and failing God. I need to fix the problem. I need to be more obedient. I need to figure out how to please God so he will stop punishing me and instead send me the blessing I need.

The punitive conclusion leaves us believing we are weak Christians and believing God is a harsh judge.

The prosperity-gospel conclusion. I must give more. That will please God more so he will in turn give me more. God's a big banker in the sky who has a guaranteed high interest rate. When I invest in him (which usually means the church), I'm told there will be a return with interest. I have to keep giving, even when I don't see the return. I have to believe that my return, my reward, will come eventually.

The prosperity-gospel conclusion leads us to believe that we must earn or even buy God's blessing.

The poverty-gospel conclusion. It is better to give than to receive. Money is the root of all evil, so as I live in lack and have less than all I desire, I'm actually growing in holiness and godly character. If I have money and resources, I must not be giving fully to the needy and the less fortunate around me. Guilt takes a deep and guiding root. To be a good Christian, I must be like Christ, who gave up everything and lived on this earth with nothing.

The poverty-gospel conclusion leaves us feeling guilty as we stand before a judgmental father.

The work-ethic conclusion. God helps those who help themselves. I must work even harder to find financial freedom. The blessing comes only from squeezing and straining and striving harder and harder. I must labor for God's approval and the slow, measured trickle of his provision to me. God demands that I pull my own weight. If I'm going to expect anything from him, it will come only by way of my own grind.

The work-ethic conclusion leads us to believe we must prove ourselves to a disciplinary father.

The formula conclusion. If I learn to spend properly, tithe faithfully, manage correctly, and exhibit self-control perfectly, then I will accurately complete the formula, and the result will be freedom.

We frustrate ourselves trying to figure out what is wrong with our formula. Should I be tithing on my gross or net income? Am I spending too much? The questions are endless, but the formula never works. The formula conclusion leads us to believe we are failures receiving an F from a mean, authoritarian God.

The false-doctrine conclusion. The Scriptures make wonderful, attractive proclamations, but they simply are not true. God does not care, and I am relegated to a life of lack and less than, layered with stress, anxiety, and disappointment. Those are my real-life circumstances. I cannot change them, and every attempt to appeal to God yields no help. I simply need to believe my circumstances, and if they contradict Scripture, so be it.

The false-doctrine conclusion leaves us believing we are rejected by an absent father.

These conclusions, or some variation or combination of them, are how we often try to rationalize God's proclaimed freedom and the reality of our financial lives. It's a pretty confusing quagmire of teaching, experience, and attempts to figure out and resolve the reality of our finances and the desire for the blessings of God. Yet none of it brings the Lord's freedom.

We must recognize that these errant teachings and understandings are not only false conclusions, but they all reduce our view of God as well. Instead of pursuing the wonder of a God whose ways are far beyond us, we reduce and limit God to our understanding and rationalizations. The mystery of a God who is our very hope is reduced to a God we think we can understand and define, no matter how hopeless that leaves us feeling. Our hope for freedom will not be found in a hopeless God.

The fact is, there is a strong element of truth in most of these conclusions. God does desire us to be in right relationship to him. Giving does open a channel of God's blessings to us and through us. The love of money is a root of all sorts of evil. Learning to be content with less than all we desire does shape our character in righteous ways. God does ask us to be good stewards both of what he has given us and of our abilities to work and manage in this world. And even though Scripture is not incorrect, it is often hard to comprehend and to gather all it teaches into one cohesive understanding. There is some truth in each of these conclusions. The problem is that they are woefully incomplete. We take actual truths and actual experiences and extrapolate them to what seem to be logical conclusions. But these logical conclusions actually are not logical at all, because they are based on this world's economy. That is, they are based on the way finances and financial systems operate in this world. God's world (or kingdom) operates differently. His financial ways are different. If we draw our conclusions with only an understanding of this world's ways, they will always fall short of the fullness of God's ways.

God's Kingdom Economy

So what are God's ways? We know some of them as giving, generosity, gratitude, worship, and blessing others. But even knowing these principles, we will still struggle if we apply them only within this world's ways, or systems of thinking. We need to ask, How does God's kingdom work? *That's* the environment I want to tackle. I will not attempt a comprehensive examination of the financial realm of this world or of God's kingdom (even if I could!), because the questions we wrestle with are more than economic or academic. They involve our everyday lives, and as Christians we realize there are deep spiritual aspects involved as well. However, all too often our attempts to answer our own questions about our financial situation lead us down an endless maze, where we analyze and reanalyze at every corner and turn. Contrary to our desire (and prayers) to be released from the stress and anxiety of finances, running the maze only adds to the frustration and raises even more questions.

I do believe the questions can be asked and addressed. I believe there are answers in the details of each circumstance and situation. However, in order to find answers to these questions, we must get radical, and I don't mean in behavior. I mean we need to get to the radical root, the very foundation of what we believe. We must establish a foundation based on the radical heart of God's love, the radical truth of his Word, the economy of his kingdom, and, yes, the reality of the world and circumstances of our lives. Floundering in a swirl of seemingly endless questions without this foundation is fruitless and frustrating. God does desire to release his righteousness, love, and provision into our lives, but we can fully realize them only when they are built on the right foundation. I will refer to this foundation as God's kingdom.

If there is a kingdom of God—and there is— then there is an economy of that kingdom as well. Accordingly, just as his kingdom is different from the earthly kingdoms or systems of this world, so is his economy different. We must understand the foundations of the economy of God's kingdom. Once we understand kingdom economics, then we can ask the questions of our life's circumstances. When we choose to operate in kingdom economics, then we will experience God's promises: the promise of freedom in all areas of our life, the promise of his faithful provision, and the reality that he cares about us and the details of our life. Within God's kingdom, he reigns and rules. In the area of finances, the promises of God are found in the economy of God and his kingdom.

In the spring of my son Kyle's senior year of high school, we took the requisite college-tour road trips. At one particular school, an economics professor led a mock class with prospective students and their parents. "Define economics," he began. After some banter, he stated that economics was simply the ability to make decisions. This struck me as odd, but as I pondered the answer, it began to make sense. In economics, we consider the situation and try to determine the cause and effect. We learn from the past, assess the present, and then attempt to determine the future.

Extend that thought process to our desire to understand God's provision in the area of finances. If we want God's kingdom economy to operate in our lives, then we need to become *kingdom* economists. The economy of this world is real. We may not think of ourselves as economists, yet simply by living in this world and experiencing this world's economy inherently makes us economists. All of us on some level know how things work, and we make decisions based on our understanding and personal experience. The problems arise when we attempt to transfer our knowledge of this world's economy to God's kingdom economic structure. Recognizing the need for a shift in perspective should not frustrate us but encourage us. Don't we want an economy that operates differently from what we are bound by in this world? We desire in our hearts to see righteousness play a more significant role in the economy of our lives. We long for a purer operation of the dynamics of an economy. We dream of living in a flow of resources where we're not always worried about running out and having to limit ourselves. We want a *different* economy.

It is for freedom that Christ sets us free. This has to include financial freedom. True freedom will not come in the brokenness of this world's economy. God invites us to live in his kingdom's economy. God invites us to understand his kingdom's foundational principles. When we know God, our Jehovah-Jireh, the Lord our Provider, then we will find the freedom for which Christ has set us free. Let's become kingdom economists!

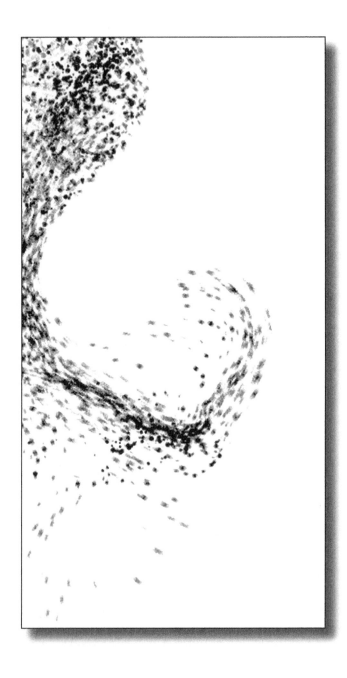

The First of the Fruit

Bring the best of the firstfruits of your soil to the house of the Lord your God. (Exodus 23:19)

"I've decided to give my entire first paycheck back to the ministry," my wife Pam informed me. "It will be kind of a firstfruits offering."

An international ministry was coming to our home state of Connecticut. There would be nearly a year of preparation for a series of significant outreach events. They would need to set up an office and full operation to prepare for and administrate this grand undertaking. Pam was hired as their treasurer. It was a great opportunity for her to contribute her skills and availability to this kingdom endeavor. And it would provide some very welcomed additional household income.

Pam's decision to consider her first paycheck a firstfruits offering reflected her gratitude to the Lord for the job itself and her overarching assurance and confidence in the Lord as her provider. In addition to our faithful practice of tithing, Pam chose to posture herself before the Lord with this additional expression of gratitude and confidence. I thought, "Sure, what a great idea." I was inspired.

The treasurer position was hourly. It was anticipated that Pam would begin working only a few hours a week, building up to full-time as the actual events drew near. As it turned out, the initial startup of the office, and specifically Pam's position, was quite demanding and required a significant amount of hours. She also assumed a biweekly paycheck, so the monthly pay period surprised her as well. As a result, that initial paycheck proved to be far more substantial (as in, a lot more money!) than she had anticipated. Moments of doubt and questions passed quickly as she held to her commitment and gave her first month's salary as a firstfruits offering.

Firstfruits is a word and a principle that appears only in Scripture and Christian language. It's quite easy to understand: it is the first of the fruit, or the first of the harvest. However, the significance of firstfruits is largely overlooked and underappreciated. Firstfruits exists in the Bible from Genesis to Revelation and is a foundational principle of our relationship with God. It is also a foundational principle of God's kingdom economy. Jesus taught us to pray, *"Your kingdom come, your will be done on earth as it is in heaven"* (Matthew 6:10). If the Lord's kingdom is to come, it will come in its fullness. It will come in all aspects, which most certainly will include foundational principles such as firstfruits. Let's take a deeper look at the economy of God's kingdom and the principle of firstfruits.

Firstfruits From the Very Beginning (Genesis 4)

Chapters 1 and 2 of Genesis paint an epic historical picture of creation. In Genesis 3 we come face to face with the world as we know it. It is now a fallen world that is less than God's desire and original design. The frailty of our human nature is evident, and the struggle of life is now woven into our existence; yet the promise of the Lord's ultimate victory is clear. Genesis 4 then begins the story of mankind outside the Garden of Eden. Our very first view into this world is the story of Cain and Abel, their response to the Lord their God, and the consequences of their heart attitudes. This story introduces us to the principle of firstfruits.

The brothers Cain and Abel each experienced the fruit of their labor. Cain, a farmer, had seen his crops yield a harvest. Abel, a shepherd, had seen his flock increase in number. Both brought their offering to the Lord, but here their paths diverged. We're told that Cain brought *some* of his harvest to offer to the Lord as a sacrifice. In contrast, Abel's offering is described as the choicest of some of his firstborn. The Lord was pleased with Abel and received his offering, but he rejected Cain's offering. This is further emphasized in Hebrews 11:4, which states that Abel's offering was received as faith and credited to him as righteousness. Cain, however, became angry because the Lord rejected his offering.

The Lord confronted Cain with a simple question. "Isn't this matter in your hands? Isn't it your choice to do what is right and consequently everything would be fine?" Instead of heeding the Lord's warning and responding to his invitation to do what was right, Cain acted upon his anger and killed his brother Abel.

What we find in this story, the very first lesson to mankind outside the garden, is the concept of firstfruits. We find a clear and simple expression of mankind's recognition that the Lord is our God and our provider. The story of Cain and Abel also declares that firstfruits is not a formula or legalistic action. Cain indeed brought the Lord an offering. However, it was not from a heart postured in gratitude to the Lord or for the Lord. This first instructional story presents us with the foundational principle of how we are to live in a fallen world and yet remain in the favor of the Lord, with his continued presence and provision.

Firstfruits as a Kingdom Principle

Firstfruits predates the laws of the Lord given through Moses. The many laws and instructions God gave Moses regarding firstfruit offerings, tithes, and sacrifices do not introduce us to the concept of firstfruits. Rather, the principle of firstfruits existed from the beginning of creation. When the Lord gathered his people to form a nation, his desire was to fashion the context where he would be their God and they would be his people. Therefore, he established laws that set understanding and parameters for his overarching principles. Firstfruits was a principle that existed within the relationship and therefore was represented throughout the laws.

By definition, firstfruits demands an understanding that we put our confidence in the Lord. At the point the *first* fruits are offered, *second* fruits may have not yet arrived. When we offer firstfruits, we say to the Lord, "We honor you for your provision, and we place our confidence and dependence on you. What you have begun, you will continue." Bringing *some* of our first harvest to the Lord is not a firstfruits offering or a firstfruits heart attitude. Pam's first paycheck was a firstfruits offering. A month later a check for an equivalent dollar amount would have been a great offering. I'm sure it would have been well received and well used, but it would not have been a firstfruits offering to the Lord her provider. The firstfruits by definition must come first.

A walk through the Bible finds the concept of firstfruits sprinkled throughout. It works its way into the laws laid out by the Lord and recorded by Moses from Exodus to Deuteronomy. It is used to describe the Israelites (Jeremiah 2:3). The Scriptures profoundly describe Jesus the Christ as the firstfruit of God's redemptive work (Romans 8; 1 Corinthians 15). We even find firstfruits used to describe the early believers, in anticipation of the full harvest yet to come (James 1:18).

However, even that quick survey of the Bible provides less than the full understanding of firstfruits, as it considers only the places where the word itself actually appears. Plus, we tend to reduce and limit the meaning of firstfruits to Old Testament sacrifices and offerings. Then we simply translate it to financial giving in our current faith expression. If we refer to it at all, we use it only to help describe and understand tithing—that it should be the first of our income, not the last or what's leftover. We further underplay the significance of firstfruits in the descriptions of Jesus and the early believers, characterizing the language as merely figurative or illustrative. What a great disservice this is to a foundational, fundamental principle of the relationship between God and his creation. Let's look deeper at a couple of other stories from the Bible that are wrapped inside this principle to help us grasp the magnitude and significance of firstfruits.

The Battle of Jericho (Joshua 5–8)

Joshua stood on a hilltop looking over at the impenetrable city of Jericho. Forty years prior he had stood looking out over this same land occupied by "giants." The Lord had promised this land to Joshua and all of Israel. What must Joshua have been thinking as he stood there? Undoubtedly, there were many times in the previous forty years of wandering in the desert he had thought about the situation before him, his mind recounting the view, the challenge of the enemy ahead of him, and the promise of the Lord behind him. How he must have longed for a different decision on that fateful day so long ago.

Joshua, as one of the twelve spies sent by Moses, had entered the Promised Land to assess the situation and conditions. Moses was preparing to lead the children of Israel into the land the Lord had set aside for them (Numbers 13). They were not rescued from the enslavement of Egypt to live in the desert. The salvation from Egypt was intended to find its fulfillment in the destination and destiny of the Promised Land.

Joshua and his fellow spies returned with their report to Moses and the people, but hope was crushed and the promise appeared to go unfulfilled. The spies' report was clear: the land indeed flowed with milk and honey (a symbol of abundance), but it was also occupied by giants, warriors, and fortified cities. Joshua and his faith-filled colleague Caleb desperately appealed for the people's confidence in their Lord. However, the other spies so successfully displaced hope with fear that Joshua and Caleb were nearly stoned to death. Consequently, the children of Israel spent forty years in the desert while a whole generation died. The next generation would inherit the Promised Land. Only Joshua and Caleb would survive to join them.

Now, after all that time, the view moved from Joshua's distant memory to the visible horizon spread out before him: the same land flowing with milk and honey, the same fortified cities, and still the same promise. There was one significant difference, though: Joshua was no longer Moses' apprentice but his successor. He would have to lead the Israelites into the promises of the Lord that he so courageously championed forty years earlier. Joshua's faith would now be tested by his leadership of the people and his humility before the Lord.

Joshua's confidence had always been in the Lord, both a generation before and still on this day. Now he encountered the "commander of the Army of the Lord," who gave him his marching orders (Joshua 5, 6). The Israelites were to march around the walled city of Jericho each day for the next six days, then on the seventh day, they were to march around the city seven times. Following that, at the sound of the trumpet blast, all the people were to give a loud war cry, and the walls would collapse before them. Charging into Jericho, they would completely destroy the city and everything in it. Jericho was to be totally devoted to the Lord. The Hebrew word translated "devoted" in Joshua 6:17 refers to the irrevocable giving over of things or persons to the Lord, often by totally destroying them. In addition, all the silver, gold, and articles of bronze and iron were to be gathered for the treasury of the Lord. Any violation of this command would bring destruction upon the individual and the whole camp of Israel.

Joshua led the people just as instructed. Jericho fell, and all was destroyed. Joshua and the nation of Israel experienced what they had so long been waiting for. The Lord was clearly going before them and leading them into the Promised Land. Obstacles and opposition need not concern them. They placed their hope and attention on faithful obedience to the Lord.

Confident in the newly experienced reality of the Lord's army going before them, Joshua and his leaders approached the next city. Ai, a small city, would not be nearly as formidable as Jericho. Joshua sent out a much smaller contingent of Israel's army for this easy conquest. But to their great surprise, the men of Ai routed the contingent, killing some of the men and driving them back in helpless retreat. How could this have happened? Joshua fell face down on the ground in grief and anguish before the Lord. His worst fears now seemed inevitable. They would be destroyed by the inhabitants of the land, and the nation of Israel would be wiped out forever. What went wrong?

"Israel has sinned," came the definitive answer from the Lord himself. Someone had taken the devoted things and stolen what belonged to the Lord. They have claimed it as their own possession. The Lord told Joshua to get up off the ground. He was to stop grieving and lamenting his fate and deal with the matter.

The Lord led Joshua through a selection process that ultimately identified the thief as the man Achan. Achan had coveted the plunder of Jericho. He had taken a robe and some silver and gold and hid it under his tent. Achan and all of his family and possessions were taken to the valley of Achor, where they were stoned and buried, along with all their possessions.

These might strike us today as awfully drastic — even disturbing — measures. Why was the response so drastic? Why was Achan's taking a handful of treasures so offensive to the Lord that it caused him to remove his favor from the Israelites when they marched against the city of Ai? Firstfruits. When we understand the principle of firstfruits, we realize Jericho was the firstfruits of the Promised Land. It was the Lord's provision that brought Israel into the Promised Land. It was a clear and undeniable fulfillment of the Lord's faithfulness to his people. That is why the Lord instructed the people to fully devote all of Jericho's treasures to the Lord either by destroying them or by bringing them into the Lord's treasury. If they touched the devoted things, they would bring destruction upon themselves. Achan means "troubler," and the valley of Achor means "the valley of trouble." Achan brought trouble upon himself and upon Israel. He had not merely touched a few trinkets or even a few treasures. No, he had stolen from the Lord. He had coveted the devoted things and taken them for his own possessions. Jericho was the Lord's, because Jericho was the firstfruits.

Once Joshua dealt with Achan's offense, the favor of the Lord returned to the nation of Israel. They conquered Ai and then city after city. Moreover, they were instructed to plunder them all, taking anything and everything they could find. After the firstfruits (Jericho) were offered to the Lord — after they honored the Lord and recognized him as their provider — the rest of the fruit came forth in abundance. Achan could have filled his tent to overflowing with treasure if he had first honored the Lord. He grasped the devoted things of the Lord instead of grasping for the Lord's favor and provision.

Just as the Lord proved himself faithful to the Israelites, so he will be faithful to us. He will bring his favor and provision as we posture ourselves in gratitude and recognize that we are completely dependent on him. We open the channel for his provision to us and through us. If we claim the firstfruits as our own, it ends the flow of provision. We are left with only the first fruit and not with the Lord of the harvest. The harvest for the Israelites was the Promised Land. As they recognized and honored the Lord with the firstfruits of Jericho, they not only received the continued presence and favor of the Lord, but they received the harvest of the Promised Land as well.

The Sacrifice of Isaac (Genesis 22)

In gaining an understanding of firstfruits, we must be careful not to make the mistake of viewing it simply as an act of obedience to God's laws. Although it is definitely an act of obedience, we must understand that this fundamental principle is much more profound than keeping rules to appease a jealous God. It is more than a formula to ensure the continued flow of provision. We need to grasp and embrace the principle of firstfruits as an act of worship. This is demonstrated for us in the challenging story of Abraham and the sacrifice of Isaac.

The story begins with God testing Abraham by instructing him to take his only son Isaac up into the mountains and sacrifice him there as a burnt offering. What could Abraham have been thinking? To us, just reading this ancient story stirs a visceral gut reaction. It strikes at our hearts and our minds. How could a loving God ever ask a father to sacrifice his son? To Abraham this command undoubtedly stirred up that same gut reaction. But we must remember that Isaac was even more than a son Abraham loved. He was the long-awaited promised one, the miracle baby born to two elderly people after waiting twenty-five years. Sarah was ninety and Abraham was a hundred years old when Isaac was born. He was the only glimmer of hope Abraham had that the inconceivably outrageous declarations of God could actually come true. The Lord had told Abraham he would be the father of nations, of so many people they could not even be counted. Now, Abraham was told by the same Lord to offer up this only son Isaac's life as a sacrifice. How could Abraham understand a command that was in direct and complete contradiction to years and years of promises and miracles? The Lord told Abraham specifically that it would be through Isaac and only through Isaac, that the promise would be fulfilled (Genesis 17). How, then, was Abraham, and how are we, to make sense of this incongruous instruction?

Abraham began by calling it worship. Abraham knew what God was asking, at least in the natural sense, and he obeyed. The very next day he headed out for the mountaintop with Isaac, two servants, and wood for the fire. Upon arriving at the place the Lord appointed, Abraham bound his son Isaac and placed him on the altar. Abraham took a knife in his hand and raised it to strike his son. At this very last moment, the Lord stopped Abraham, but not because a loving God could not ask Abraham to go through with this sacrificial act of worship. No, the Lord stopped Abraham specifically because he *was* willing to go through with it. He was willing to lay down the miraculous gift *from* the Lord in obedience *to* the Lord. Abraham demonstrated his faith that the Lord would provide. He had provided Isaac, and he would be faithful to fulfill all of his promises.

At that moment Abraham looked up and saw a ram caught in a thicket. He sacrificed the ram in the place of his son. This was the first sacrificial lamb and was a pointer toward things to come. Then the Lord reconfirmed his promises. Because Abraham had not withheld Isaac, the Lord would indeed bless Abraham with the fulfillment of all of his promises. Abraham would not have just one son but would be the father of nations. Abraham then named the place where these truths were revealed and realized, Jehovah-Jireh, "the Lord Provides."

Isaac was the firstfruits. In order for Abraham to be the father of many nations, of countless people, there would have to be one who was born first. Isaac was the firstborn and thus the firstfruits. If Abraham looked at Isaac simply as the result of the long, faithful, twenty-five-year wait for the promise of God to be fulfilled, surely he would have clung to the gift of Isaac. He would have protected him with all he had. He would have treasured him and never let him go. Without the gift of faith, our tendency, and I believe Abraham's as well, is to grasp and cling to everything, especially the good things the Lord provides in answer to our prayers and in accord with his promises.

But firstfruits is an act of worship whereby we honor God and his demonstrated faithfulness. And God is not simply faithful in his ability to provide a little; rather, he is faithful in his character. He is not simply able to muster up part of an answer or part of a promise or *some* provision. He is faithful to his word, no matter how grand, or outrageous, or inconceivable it may appear to us. Our act of worship through understanding and offering firstfruits allows the Lord to be our Jehovah-Jireh, the Lord who provides. Worshiping through firstfruits opens the flow of God's faithfulness and heaven's resources to fulfill the Lord's promises, provide for our needs, and release heaven's blessings to earth. A firstfruits offering as an act of worship turns our attention from the provision we've received to the provider himself.

Abraham did not need to sacrifice Isaac to appease God. God was asking Abraham to open a flow of heaven's redemptive purposes for mankind through Isaac and ultimately through Jesus himself, as a descendent of Abraham and Isaac. The firstfruits offering of Isaac (including the sacrificial ram) was an act of worship. The firstfruits offering opened the flow for the full harvest to come. That flow continues to this day, and it will continue into eternity.

(A much more comprehensive look at Genesis 22 and the name and meaning of Jehovah-Jireh will be addressed in chapter 7. For now, this story is presented as part of our understanding of firstfruits.)

Jesus as Firstfruits

Now that we are equipped with a better understanding of the principle of firstfruits, let's look at the profound declarations that Jesus himself is the firstfruits of God's redemption. From the victory over sin to the redemption of all of creation struggling under the weight of the fall, Jesus Christ is the central figure, the answer, and the hope of the Lord and his kingdom.

And we know that in all things God works for the good of those who love him, who have been called according to his purpose. For those God foreknew he also predestined to be conformed to the likeness of his son, that he might be the firstborn among many brothers. (Romans 8:28-29)

But Christ has indeed been raised from the dead, the firstfruits of those who have fallen asleep [died]. (1 Corinthians 15:20)

Jesus is described as the firstborn (firstfruits) of many brothers and sisters. He stands not only as a firstfruit of salvation but also of several other promises: that all things work together for the predestined purposes of the Lord, that there is victory over sin and death, and that the sons and daughters of God will embody his redemption of all his creation. The apostle Paul, the author of these two books, brings Romans 8 to a great poetic climax, declaring that what God birthed through Jesus, his firstborn of redemption, is now an unstoppable reality. Nothing and no one — no power or situation, no circumstance or condition — can block the flow of his redemption promises. Jesus is the firstborn, and once the firstfruit has come forth, the destiny of the fullness of his victory and the Lord's promises will indeed follow (Romans 8:35-39).

Scripture refers to Jesus as the second Adam (1 Corinthians 15:47). In the perspective of God's redemptive plan, we also see Jesus as the second Isaac. It may be difficult for us to understand the Lord's command to Abraham to offer Isaac as a sacrifice. We discussed how this was an act of worship and that Isaac was the firstfruits of the promise the Lord had repeatedly given Abraham. For Abraham and Isaac, the Lord provided a sacrificial lamb. However, as Jesus brings to us the fullness and fulfillment of that great promise first given to Abraham, he himself *is* the sacrificial lamb. The very story we may find offensive (the Lord asking Abraham to offer his son Isaac as a blood sacrifice) we actually embrace in Jesus' death (God the Father offering his son Jesus as a blood sacrifice).

It's important to recognize that Jesus was not simply raised from the dead but was resurrected. He wasn't raised from the dead and restored to a pre-death, mortal life. Rather, he was resurrected into the glorified reality of eternal life. He was the first to experience it, the firstfruits of the greatest of all harvests. Consider that upon Jesus' resurrection, he would never die again. All others raised to life were restored to their mortal lives, to eventually die again (the wages of sin). Jesus, however, was resurrected, becoming the firstborn of eternal life. Lazarus needed the stone rolled away to let him out of the tomb. The stone in front of Jesus' tomb was rolled away to reveal that Jesus was no longer there. When he appeared to Mary, the disciples, and many others in those few weeks following his resurrection, Jesus was recognizable and yet not always recognized. Something had changed. He was visible and physical. He showed people his nail-pierced hands and feet. He ate actual food, and yet he would appear and disappear behind closed doors. The physical laws governing this world didn't limit him (Luke 24; John 21). Jesus is the firstborn of the resurrection, the firstfruits of many brothers and sisters, the greatest of all harvests.

We must remember that Jesus was not only the sacrificial lamb (laying down his life on the cross), but he was also the firstborn of the resurrection. He was not only victorious over sin and death but also was the firstfruits of the fullness of redemption. The principle of firstfruits, which predates the law and is representative of the relationship between the Creator God and his creation, is an integral reality in the person of Jesus and the saving plan for us through Jesus the Christ. *"But Christ has indeed been raised from the dead, the firstfruits of those who have fallen asleep [died]"* (1 Corinthians 15:20). Our hope for eternal life is predicated on Jesus' life, death, and resurrection as the firstfruits of eternal life.

Applying Firstfruits

It's one thing to gain an understanding of firstfruits but quite another to put it into practice. We can

47

understand and even agree with it, but how do we apply it in our lives, in our day, and in our culture? Most of us are not farmers. We don't have young lambs or bushels of grain to offer. Even if we did, how would we offer them? We don't have altars for burnt offerings before the Lord. Do we sell them and give the money to the Lord by giving it to the church?

The most obvious, natural, and consistent practice of firstfruits is the tithe. We will discuss tithing in detail later, but for now let's simply state that it is the practice identified in the Old Testament of giving the first 10 percent of our provision to the Lord. I use the word *provision* because when the law was established, provision could have been anything from harvest to currency. We need to pick our words carefully. Carrying the practice forward to today, provision is overwhelmingly expressed in currency. Understanding firstfruits reminds us that tithing is not a God tax for which we hope we have enough money left over to pay. Firstfruits positions our hearts in a posture of gratitude and trust in the Lord. When we thank him with the first of our provision, we declare to the Lord and to ourselves that our confident hope is in the Lord's faithful provision. Tithing is a clear, simple, and easily understood expression of the foundational firstfruits principle.

Tithing is a wonderfully adequate embrace of firstfruits. However, the heart attitudes expressed in the principle of firstfruits—that of gratitude and trust—should permeate every aspect of our lives. If we decide that whenever we have a fresh flow of provision we will express our gratitude and trust in the Lord through giving firstfruit offerings, then there are endless opportunities and ways to honor the Lord. Firstfruits may be expressed many ways, not simply with monetary gifts. For Abraham it was actually laying down his son, who was the first of the promised sons to come. For Joshua and the Israelites, Jericho was the first city of the Promised Land.

I began this chapter with the illustration of Pam offering her first paycheck as firstfruits. We actually have taken this same specific step on a couple of occasions. Pursuing and practicing firstfruits giving has helped us to maintain grateful hearts and a proper perspective through honoring the Lord whenever we receive a new or different provision. The circumstances vary for every reader, so the kinds and number of opportunities also will vary from person to person. To encourage you and possibly broaden your perspective, let me share a few other ways we have practiced firstfruits.

The first time I recall a desire to press into this principle was many years ago while working for a large corporation. We had always tithed faithfully, but we began to ask ourselves whether tithing was the only expression of firstfruits. How could we bring a firstfruits offering beyond tithing when we only collected a steady paycheck week after week? As we pondered this question, we realized the one variation from the steady paycheck was an annual raise. Although not a guarantee, it was expected in my position at my corporation. We decided we wanted to view these annual raises as new provision from the Lord. Sure raises may have been common practice from my employer, but they were also the Lord's provision to us. We decided to offer the full amount of the raise, in addition to our tithe, for one full year. Our desire was to thank our Lord for raises and to put our trust in his provision for us, whether this came through ongoing raises or any other means he chose. As my annual review approached, we began to pray for a sizable increase. I recall feeling freedom to pray for a significant raise without feeling it was a selfish prayer. Sure enough, a couple months later at my annual review I received a very healthy raise. With the decision already made, we joyfully and faithfully added the raise to our tithe offering for the following year. It was an entrée for us into deeper expressions of firstfruits and a deeper understanding of our relationship with our Jehovah-Jireh.

In addition, we have made sure to give firstfruits offerings from inheritance we received and the handful of stocks we've owned. One stock in particular has been exceedingly prosperous, and we recognized how extraordinary that was. Believing in firstfruits, we immediately sold a small percentage of the stock and gave the full amount as an offering. It was yet another opportunity to thank the Lord.

We don't approach these faith steps as a formula. Rather, they are very natural, comfortable, and tangible expressions of gratitude to the Lord, as well as a clear declaration of our confident trust in his provision. Our peace for the present and hope for the future rest in our relationship with the Lord, not in what we have, what we can acquire, or what we can cling to. Our highest priority is to lean into our relationship with God in every way possible.

One of our most dramatic experiences with firstfruits was not directly in the realm of finances. We were very much settled into a wonderful neighborhood, raising our boys and enjoying our community very much. While on a lunchtime walk one day, a "For Sale" sign caught my attention. I had passed the house many times, and I was always curious about the layout because the house was a little unique. Although we were not in the market for a new house or had any intention to move, Pam humored my curiosity, and we took the opportunity to look inside. Immediately upon entering the house with our realtor, the Lord expressed his plans to us, which went far beyond our simple curiosity. Both of us individually received a strong impression of the house full of people in all manner of ministry and community. It would be a place to host our belief and passion for God's kingdom to come into this world. Unmistakably, we were to purchase the home, move in, and open the doors. It didn't hurt that the house was beautiful. My intrigue about this uniquely shaped house was met with delight when we saw how the open architecture was an ideal setting for both small and large gatherings.

However, we did not want to move. Our boys had just started a new year in a school and school system we and they liked very much. Moving over only one town still meant new schools, new neighbors, new playmates, and a new environment for all of us. It would mean saying good-bye to a full complement of things we thoroughly liked and enjoyed. Why would we want to give those up? In addition, the housing market had been flat for a decade, and this upgrade would come with a significant increase in cost. Yet we remained convinced the Lord was directing the move, and we soon found him not only directing but also orchestrating the move. We found ourselves using savings and inheritance to purchase the new house while not immediately selling our current home, thus actually carrying two homes for a period of time.

Remember that job I mentioned at the beginning of this chapter that Pam had just begun for an international ministry? At the time of this house purchase, the large-scale evangelistic festivals were still eight months away. However, the organization regularly brought in trainers, developers, and promoters to prepare for these festivals. We decided that if this new house was a provision from the Lord, it was his to use and ours to steward. We would rely on him to provide us with the ability to afford and maintain it, and we would express our gratitude and our trust in him. With friends' help, we furnished the four bedrooms and the living room and offered the new house to the international ministry Pam worked for as a resource for their many out-of-town guests. For eight months while we remained in our old house, the new house served as a warm inn for many visitors, and it saved the organization a lot of money by avoiding hotel costs.

It was a firstfruits offering to the Lord. We postured ourselves in gratitude and service. When the festivals were done and the organization moved on to their next location, we moved into our new home. By that time, our boys had finished the school year in their current school without having to change midyear. We also were able to sell our old house on our own in a market that, after a decade of stagnation, suddenly made a sharp upswing. That increase more than covered the extra expense of carrying two homes for those eight months. Now we continue to have the privilege of living in this beautiful home. In the years since that initial firstfruits offering, we have used the home in a myriad of ways. We remain very aware of where the house came from, why we are here, and how we are to steward this resource for the Lord. It is one of our delights in the testimony to the principle of firstfruits.

I share these stories as encouragement. For us, firstfruits is not just a good principle. It is a reality we experience and a principle to which we are committed. It transcends finances and formulas. It is the blessing of a genuine relationship with a loving Jehovah-Jireh, the Lord who provides. Everyone's situation will be different. I encourage you to lean into the principle of firstfruits. Ask the Lord and ask yourself if there are ways and opportunities for you to exercise this foundational principle. I encourage you to move beyond formulas of tithing to postures of humility, gratitude, and trust. I suspect all of us have ways to make firstfruits offerings. For example, do you grow a garden? Most people I know who garden get to a point when the harvest actually comes that they can't consume all the produce at the time that it's ripe. They take bags of squash and zucchini to their workplace or neighbors. Many enjoy this wonderful heart attitude of sharing. So why not take the *first* handful of tomatoes or your *first* ear of corn and offer those? Before tasting the fresh sweetness of the fruit of your labor, why not give that away with a heart declaration, not only to bless someone else but also to thank the Lord for his provision?

What are the ways the Lord blesses you? Are there gifts, talents, or resources you operate in that you can thank the Lord for in a firstfruits expression? Prayerfully consider your life and the Lord's provision. Remember, it's not a formula but a foundational principle in which God's kingdom economy flows. I invite you to experience heaven's flow.

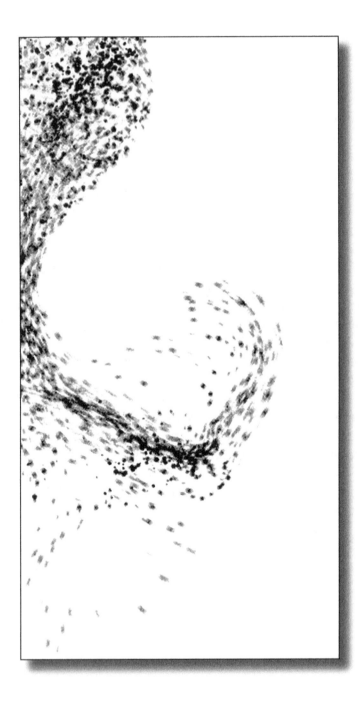

Flow

For the jar of flour was not used up and the jug of oil did not run dry, in keeping with the word of the LORD spoken by Elijah. (1 Kings 17:16)

Firstfruits by the very nature of the word itself implies that there is more to follow. If there is a first, then the expectation is that there will be a second, third, or even more. Yet if we could always see the second, third, and more, then our embrace of the principle of firstfruits would be more an act of obedience than a step of faith. After all, *"faith is being sure of what we hope for and certain of what we do not see"* (Hebrews 11:1). When our giving is primarily out of obedience, it lacks the spirit of gratitude and the declaration that our hope is in the Lord himself. It can fail to be true worship.

Recall the first story we discussed in the last chapter. Cain brought an offering out of obedience, but he lacked a grateful heart, and God rejected it. Firstfruits is easier to see in hindsight, when we can also see the second, third, and more. However, most often at the point of firstfruits, faith is required to believe that the second, third, or more will actually follow. Firstfruits may not feel like it's just the first. It often feels like it's *all* the fruit. Therefore, firstfruits cannot simply be a measured response of obedience. It is the recognition of a greater reality; that is, that provision, both what is in hand and what will come, is dependent on the Lord. It is also a declaration that God's goodness and faithfulness will continue.

The Bottomless Jar (1 Kings 17)

Faith in the unseen but never-ending provision of the Lord is wonderfully depicted in our introduction to Elijah. The first story in the Bible of this great prophet reads like a parable or fable, but it is an actual historical account from ancient Israel chronicled in 1 Kings 17. We first meet Elijah as he confronts Ahab, king of Israel, with a prophetic word: there would be no rain or dew in the land for years until and unless Elijah gave the command. Elijah not only confronted the king with a dramatic declaration, but he also placed himself above the king as God's authority and mouthpiece. The Lord then immediately led Elijah into hiding to protect his life. The hiding place was both a place of protection and provision. There was a stream for him to drink from during the very drought that he prophesied. But water cannot sustain a man forever, so the Lord sent ravens to bring him bread and meat twice a day. The Lord's provision for Elijah is reminiscent of his provision of manna for the Israelites in the desert.

Eventually the drought even dried up the stream, so the Lord directed Elijah to a town where he would cross paths with a widow. The Lord told Elijah the widow would provide for him. When he met her, Elijah asked for bread, but she informed him that all she had left was a handful of flour and a spot of oil. She was on her way home to make one final small meal for her son and herself. After that, she was certain they would starve to death. Elijah instructed the widow to proceed with her plans but to first make him a small loaf of bread. Then her flour and oil would not run out. The widow proceeded as Elijah instructed her, and she had enough to feed Elijah, her son, and herself for that meal and continually. The jar of flour was never empty, and the bottle of oil never ran out until the day the rains returned to water the land.

If you were the woman in this story, at the very end of your provision with absolutely no prospects for any resupply, what would your perspective be? How would you feel? The Scriptures actually say that prior to Elijah approaching the woman, the Lord had already instructed her to provide for him. Even still, if you had nothing with which to provide, how could you provide for him? We have discussed firstfruits, but what about a broader understanding of giving and receiving? How do we measure and ensure that we are faithful in what the Lord desires of us? What is the heart attitude God desires that would cause us, like this woman, to give away even what little we have? Furthermore, why would God ask us for the meager amounts we have to offer when he is the Lord of the universe?

It's easy to read a story about how God miraculously provides and simply accept it. We may pause to say, "Wow, isn't God amazing," but then we move on. We can forget that we are reading the story in hindsight, with the wonderfully miraculous faithfulness of God already revealed. We may fail to mine the deeper revelations of such a dramatic encounter between God and his people by not placing ourselves in this real-life story, seeing and feeling the emotions and steps of faith that are taken without the benefit of knowing the outcome. Why didn't the woman cling to that last precious handful of flour and drop of oil? How could she trust the Lord and the Lord's voice through Elijah? What was the Lord asking of her? What truths of God's kingdom economy did she step into?

We may view this dramatic story as an isolated historical miracle. We may see it solely as God's provision to his chosen one, Elijah. However, when we view the story only in light of God's favor to Elijah, we miss two powerful kingdom realities. First, we separate Elijah from ourselves, creating two categories of people: those whom God choses and therefore walks with and divinely works in their lives; and the rest of us, who cannot depend on divine intervention. James 5 rejects this notion by declaring that Elijah was a man just like us. Second, with this view we miss the operating kingdom principle so beautifully demonstrated in the story, the principle the Lord desires for us to grasp. That is one reason the story is preserved and shared with us. Let's not separate the miracle of the lasting flour and oil from any principle of the provision and economy of God's kingdom. Let's look at this story through both these lenses: how it applies to us, and what kingdom principle it reveals.

God unmistakably brought his kingdom into the circumstances facing Elijah, the woman and her child, the drought in the land, and the end of her food. Instead of viewing the outcome from hindsight, let's look at kingdom principles that are revealed inside this dramatic encounter with God's provision. The story begins with the clear observation that God is actively involved in providing for all of them. He is not oblivious to the circumstances, but rather he is active for their good in the midst of the circumstances. Both Elijah and the woman also are listening to the Lord and willing to respond in faith and obedience, even when the outcome is uncertain. We could even say that the outcome is quite certain. Without God's intervention, the provision will run out and they will all surely starve. So, we cannot understand their actions solely by what they see and what they know in the natural.

What would have happened if the woman had said, "I don't have anything to give you above what I need for myself and my son?" What would have happened if she told Elijah she would bake the bread for herself and her son and if there was any left over she would generously offer it to him? Would there have been any left over? What would have happened if she had refused to give anything to Elijah? Even if the flow didn't run out this time, it surely would at the next meal. How long would the flour have lasted if the woman had attempted to ration it? This was a matter of life and death. What was Elijah asking for and willing to take from this woman? What happened when the woman agreed to first bake some bread for Elijah? The widow chose to hold loosely what she had rather than cling to it. In so doing, she experienced God's kingdom economics.

Let's look at the kingdom principles of giving and receiving. Let's look at operating with *open hands* rather than *clinging* to what is ours, what we need, and what has been given to us. Let's look at the difference between measuring what we have and trusting in a continuous supply. To examine and articulate these kingdom principles, we'll look at an incident from Jesus' life where these same dynamics of God's economy were experienced: the feeding of the five thousand.

"You Feed Them" (Luke 9:10-17)

Matthew, Mark, Luke, and John all record the inspiring story of Jesus' compassionate and miraculous act of meeting the very immediate need of feeding a massive crowd numbering five thousand men. The actual number easily could have been ten thousand or more when women and children are included. The crowd followed Jesus all day. As Jesus taught and ministered, the crowd grew and grew while the hours passed. Late in the day the disciples approached Jesus about dismissing the crowd so they could return home or at least go to nearby villages to find something to eat. Quite likely they were expressing their concern for the people, as they too were growing weary from the long day without food. They would welcome a good meal, so the crowd must need the same. "Jesus, as long as you keep teaching and ministering, no one will leave. See, the crowd keeps growing. We think it would be a good idea to wrap it up and send them on their way."

"You feed them," Jesus replied. *You* feed them? This was not practical. It was preposterous. Obviously the disciples did not have food to feed anyone, let alone a huge crowd. They even critiqued how much it would cost and how foolish it would be to attempt to buy enough food for such a mass of people. "*You* feed them?" How were they to respond to Jesus? Jesus had made some outlandish statements over the last couple years, statements that made no sense, and this too was completely absurd. The disciples had asked a practical question about a real situation. Jesus wasn't foolish, or naïve, so what was he asking of them?

A quick search of the crowd turned up one boy's lunch of two fish and five rolls of bread. This may have been a big lunch for a boy, but it seemed worthless to the charge that Jesus had just given them to feed everyone.

The disciples were defeated, but Jesus simply had them instruct the people to sit down on the ground in groups of around fifty people each. Jesus did not berate the disciples. He did not say, "What were you thinking, bringing me this measly lunch? What are we going to do with this? How is this going to solve our problem?" He did not regress into despair and plead with God in desperation. He simply instructed the disciples to prepare the people for a meal.

What happened next revealed Jesus' perspective on the whole situation. It was very different from the disciples' perspective or what ours would have been. All four Gospels record that Jesus took the boy's lunch, lifted it to heaven, and thanked the Father for his provision. Jesus then broke the bread and through the disciples began to distribute it to the crowd. Here, the multiplication began, breaking the bread and passing it around and breaking the bread and passing it around until thousands of people had their fill. The disciples then gathered up the leftovers and filled twelve baskets. I can see each disciple taking a basket and gathering up leftovers. Twelve disciples were each left holding a basketful of witness to the abundance of God's resources.

What happened that day is often referred to as a miracle of multiplication. Although this accurately describes what transpired, I don't believe it fully captures all the Lord demonstrated. Jesus' desire was for the disciples to feed everyone. Obviously, they could not do this from what they had, and they did not have the ability to provide it. They had not previously received an abundance from the Lord, which they had stored up for such a time as this, when they could share from the overflow of what they had accumulated. They couldn't give what they didn't have. Nor could they somehow make it happen in the moment. They couldn't scramble and come up with enough money or food to provide for the need before them. But, "You feed them" was Jesus' instruction.

Flow

Jesus took the boy's lunch, held it up to heaven, and thanked the Father for it. Instead of lamenting over not having enough, instead of accusing God the Father of not providing all that they needed, instead of dismissing God and trying to make something happen in his own strength and ability (or the disciples'), Jesus took what he had and gave thanks. He said, "Father, thank you for what you have given us." Thanksgiving was Jesus' response. He knew that a boy's lunch could not feed thousands of people. He also knew the Father was not ignorant of the circumstances. Therefore, if this was what the Father had provided, then it would be more than adequate. So he began to distribute the boy's lunch, using what the Father had provided. When Jesus thanked the Father, he opened a flow of heaven's resources to the need before him. The boy's lunch may not have been adequate, but the resources of heaven were more than adequate. The Father's provision was more than adequate. Jesus thanked his Father, and the disciples began to feed the crowd. Heaven's resources began to flow.

Our perspective is most often based on what we already have. Even if we credit God for it, we measure what we have and what he has provided. We label what we can see as the Lord's provision. Then, when we see needs before us, whether for ourselves or for others, we feel the obligation to meet those needs from what we have. We think we must meet the need either from what we have stored up or from what we can gather. The stories of feeding the five thousand and Elijah and the widow provide us with a fundamentally different perspective. What we have in hand is not how we should measure the Lord's provision. If we believe our wonderful heavenly Father is our provider, then we must look to his provision.

I believe fundamentally that giving and receiving are simply the wrong measures because they place us at the center. The Lord gives freely, and it is wonderful to receive from him. He is a great provider and the great Father of blessings. It is good and right to receive and enjoy what he gives us. It is also in God's very nature to give. As we are made in his image and represent him, it is good for us to give as well. The Scriptures say it is better to give than to receive (Acts 20:35). The Scriptures also say freely we have received, freely give (Matthew 10:8). So giving and receiving are normal and wonderful dimensions of our lives that we should practice with humility and godly hearts. They are integral parts of our relationship with the Father. However, the problem with using receiving and giving as measures is that this places *us* at the center point of the equation. How much can *I* receive? How much can *I* give? Even when we are giving and receiving with proper heart attitudes, the center of the equation remains us, which will always be a limiting factor. *We* can give only so much. *We* can receive and store only so much.

The mistake comes when we believe that for us to receive God's provision and give from his provision, we must carry the inventory ourselves. Like a large distribution center of God's resources, we feel we need to have it in our possession. Inventory is good, and wise, godly stewardship is expected. Carelessness and foolishness wastefully depletes what the Lord has provided to us. However, we cannot measure God's provision based on the size of our inventory.

Instead of measuring God's provision through what we can obtain and what we can give, we should focus on how much we can allow his provision to flow through us. The simple, unassuming, and unpretentious word *flow* best describes our active partnership with God's heart and resources. God invites us to be channels of his love and blessings, including his provision.

The miracle of Jesus and the disciples feeding the five thousand demonstrates the kingdom principles of firstfruits and flow. Jesus took the boy's lunch and thanked God for his provision. This was an act of firstfruits. Jesus was thankful for what he had and offered it to God with a full understanding that after the firstfruits would come the full and more-than-adequate provision to meet the need. Firstfruits is what we bring. It is not the miracle itself. The miracle of multiplication is what follows. Firstfruits is our posture before the Lord that allows for and even calls forth the miracle. With a thankful heart, Jesus opened a channel of God's provisional flow. Once the flow was opened, it did not run out until everyone had his or her fill.

Let's remember this is not a parable. It is an account of an actual experience, so let's consider the setting and details a little more. After Jesus gave thanks to God, did the floodgate of heaven open and a truckload of fish and bread fall to the earth? No. Instead, as Jesus and the disciples broke the bread and distributed it, heaven's provision continued to fill the baskets until all the needs were met. I've always been curious as to exactly how and where the multiplication was happening. If I were one of the disciples, I would have been intently studying the bread and the baskets, trying to see or figure it out. We don't know how it happened, but we do know it happened in an endless, multiplying flow, not in a one-time, heavenly dump.

Consider this: What if the disciples had grown weary from handing out the baskets of food? After feeding a few thousand people, I can imagine that their backs ached. What would have happened if they had sat down and said, "That's enough. We're tired and we can't do anymore"? Would the multiplying flow have continued? Would fish and loaves of bread have begun to pile up and overflow the baskets? No. I believe from our window into the story, the multiplication would have ceased. The flow continued as they continued to distribute the food. And what about the opposite? What if people from the nearby villages joined the throngs after hearing about this miraculous feast? If the disciples had the strength to continue, would the multiplication have continued? Once Jesus opened the flow from the storehouses of heaven, what would cause the divine flow to cease?

The principle of flow is the means by which we connect with the provision of God. Firstfruits opens the way, and flow describes the method. Flow brings us personally into the process. It allows us to actively partner with heaven without being at the center of the equation. It's not about what we can receive or what we can give but rather about how much we make ourselves an open channel for the *flow* of God's resources. The disciples probably never had more than one basket of food at a time, but who knows how many basketfuls must have passed through their hands that day. Measuring what we can get and what we can give limits heaven's resources. Flow opens the limitless storehouse of Jehovah-Jireh, the Lord of provision.

Flow should not be a foreign concept to the believer. It is clearly understood in many aspects and attributes of God and his kingdom. However, we often feel that different principles must apply to the realm of provision than from all other aspects of God. For example, we easily understand the principle of flow with the kingdom resource of hope. We don't measure how much hope we have before we decide whether we can give it away. And yet we know that as we share hope with someone else, we don't deplete our own reservoir of hope. In fact, when we share hope, our own hope usually rises, or increases, as well. There might be seasons when we have little hope or when hope is overflowing, but we don't try to manage our hope by measuring how much hope we have received or can give, as if it were a limited commodity. The same is true with love, peace, encouragement, joy, and other aspects of God and his kingdom. When we pursue our relationship with God, we allow his life and kingdom's reality into our lives in all its fullness. "May your kingdom come, may your will be done," is Jesus' instruction not only for our prayer but also for our understanding for how God's kingdom is available to us. That includes the provision of the Lord.

A Channel for Flow (2 Kings 4)

Flow is probably most clearly represented in another Old Testament account of a different widow and her sons, as her resources were running dry. For this particular woman, it came through the prophet Elijah's protégé Elisha. We find the story in 2 Kings 4. One of Elisha's followers had died, and his widowed wife had been left with no means to provide for herself and her sons. When she came to Elisha, creditors were threatening to take her sons away and place them in servitude. The only provision she had left was a small jar of olive oil. Elisha instructed her to gather all the containers she could find; and not only was she to collect her own, but she also was to boldly ask her neighbors for every possible container they could spare. She was to retreat into her house with her small jar of oil, the empty containers, and her sons and close the door behind her. Elisha instructed her to pour the olive oil into the containers one by one. As she began to pour from the small amount of olive oil she had, she filled the first container. Her sons brought her the second container, and she filled it. Then she filled the third, the fourth, and every container until no more were available. Upon filling the final container, the oil stopped "flowing." The woman then sold the very large supply of oil she now possessed. She was able to pay off her creditors and still have plenty with which to live.

The principles we previously articulated in the story of Jesus feeding the five thousand are seen plainly here in this encouraging recounting of God's faithfulness. As the channel of God's provision was opened through faith and action, flow continued as long as there were jars to contain it. They were not filled in one miraculous moment. The small jar of oil, which seemed insignificant and obviously insufficient to meet the needs of her family, was the channel for the flow of God's provision. As they believed God and used the provision before them, it met their needs not only in the moment but also for their future as well. Flow is not to be measured. In understanding flow we recognize the limitless supply from which it comes.

It is so easy to get in the way of flow. We try to measure it. We try to dam it up so that we can create a reservoir. We view flow from our limited perspective and believe it's too meager and insufficient. The problem is not the flow but our perspective. We are looking at a snapshot, a moment in time, the only part we can see. We determine that this is all we have, and it's not enough. We question whether more will come and how more could possibly come. When we focus on the undesirable consequences that will surely result when there's nothing left, it's as if we're looking at a specific point in a river while wearing blinders. We see only the water right in front of us at that particular moment. We would be concerned only if we did not understand that the flow of water will continue to pass through our focal point. Remember one of the principles we've already stated is that the economy of God's kingdom is different from the economy of this world. We need to be economists of kingdom economics rather than of this world's economic systems. Flow is the method by which the resources of heaven are made available and delivered to us. Understanding flow allows us to be thankful for what we have and confident that even though it may not be sufficient, the Lord is God almighty, the all-sufficient one. His resources are limitless. We don't need to have them in our tight grip to know that they are available. In fact, the very act of gripping chokes the flow. The woman feeding Elijah had to release her grip on her seemingly last provision in order to feed him and open the flow.

Flow is the means by which God's resource moves from simply being available to actually supplying our needs. When we grip, grasp, and cling to what we have, we stop the flow. This is true even when what we have is a direct gift from the Lord. Recall the story of Abraham offering Isaac on the altar. Isaac was God's gift, the miracle son, and the offspring through whom God's promises would be realized. If Abraham had clung to his treasured Isaac, he would have stopped the flow from the Lord that would bring forth that very promise. Abraham had to consciously place his trust in the giver (God) above the gift from God (Isaac). In so doing, he shifted from a worldly mindset of receiving and clinging to a kingdom mindset of trusting and releasing.

From Overflow to Flow

This is not a formula. We don't force the hand of God by our action or inaction. The principle of flow begins with faith that directs our actions. The woman believed the Lord would provide for her even if she used her last bit of provision to feed Elijah. Jesus believed the Father's resources were sufficient for feeding thousands. Abraham most assuredly did not know how offering Isaac on the altar could possibly fulfill the promises God had made, but he loosened his grip nonetheless.

These are all actions dictated by faith that encourage and inspire; but these accounts are all ancient, and they involve other people's lives and circumstances. As simple as it is to see and even understand these great Bible stories, the faith principles they teach us are often quite difficult to apply to our own lives. Our bills exceed our checking account. Our desires and even needs seem to go unfulfilled because we simply cannot meet our obligations. When there is no flow, how can we let actions that seem like careless faith trump our responsibilities and obligations?

Good stewardship, meeting obligations, and being wisely responsible are good and godly approaches in everything we do. We can never excuse ourselves from such conduct. The question, then, is how do we hold these two realities in tension, especially when they appear to be at odds with each other? The shift I am attempting to articulate here is from *overflow* to *flow*. The mindset of this world's economy is governed by overflow. We gladly give from our overflow. Needs around us may trigger our compassion and our desire to help. We value life and God's love for others. We want to give. We want to help. We want to be a source of hope and an ambassador of God's kingdom. However, if we are operating from a worldly economic perspective, we desire extra so that we can give from that overflow. Overflow is good, but very few of us have it or feel we have it. And more importantly, it is difficult to determine what is necessary and what should be considered overflow. Often we feel we need more, even if it's just a little more. There are plenty of legitimate needs and good uses for what we have, so it is difficult to actually get to a place of excess or overflow. I define giving from the overflow as the spirit of philanthropy. We freely give from the extra of what we have.

In stark contrast, the kingdom mindset realizes there *is* enough — even extra, even an abundance. It may not reside in our worldly coffers, but we are citizens of the kingdom of God. More importantly, we are sons and daughters of the King and have access to all of his limitless provision. A kingdom economist understands that an overflow of our own resources is not required; rather, what is needed are faith and actions that will open the flow of those heavenly resources. An overflow mindset places us at the fountainhead. That is, we give from our resources. Understanding flow accurately places our confidence in the Lord as our fountainhead, regardless of what we see or have at the moment.

Overflow is a heart attitude that meets our needs first and then considers others. Flow is faith and confidence that our needs are already met in God's full provision and faithfulness to us. Therefore, our starting point does not even begin with us and what we have.

It's revealing that a quick look at the occurrences of the word *overflow* in the Bible shows that it rarely has reference to money or resources. By and large, the word is used to express an overabundance of spiritual wellsprings.

> *For out of the overflow of the heart the mouth speaks. (Matthew 12:34)*
>
> *...so that you may overflow with hope by the power of the Holy Spirit. (Romans 15:13)*
>
> *Their overflowing joy and their extreme poverty welled up in rich generosity. (2 Corinthians 8:2)*
>
> *...the grace that is reaching more and more people may cause thanksgiving to overflow to the glory of God. (2 Corinthians 9:12)*

Obviously, the kingdom overflows, but the abundance that wells up into springs of living water is the essence of God and his nature, not merely his resources. "Lord, bless me that I may meet my needs and overflow in blessing to others" is a fine prayer; however it does not open the door for the fullness of God's kingdom economy. Jesus taught us to pray, "May your kingdom come." Overflow is a blessing, while flow opens a channel to a new reality, to a completely different economy. Flow allows for the miraculous. It allows God's kingdom to transform this world. Flow places our confidence and faith in God, which releases us from the weight and burden of meeting our own needs.

I have a dear friend who travels the world as an itinerant minister. He lives a lifestyle that he describes as "living by faith." He and his wife and family embody this lifestyle as genuinely as anyone I know. Where he travels, what he ministers, and how they live depends daily on his walk with and direction from his heavenly Father. I have heard him say that when things get really desperate financially, he'll say to his wife, "Honey, we're going to have to give our way out of this one!" His bubbling laugh follows, giving a sense of humor to what he is saying even as he expresses a sincerely true perspective. Neither he nor I would consider this a complete doctrine, but it does reveal a heart that understands he's a true son of the Father. He lives in the flow of heaven's provision.

Understanding flow allows us to shift our attention and focus away from what we have, what we don't have, what we can get, and even what we can give. Instead, through praise and thanksgiving, our perspective shifts to a confident faith and expectation in our heavenly Father, his sufficiency, and even his abundance. When we join him and become a channel of his love and provision, we open a flow of God's kingdom to this earth.

We have discussed the fundamental principles of firstfruits and flow. Now let's address the application of these principles. What are the practical steps for giving, generosity, and trusting in God? Let's discuss how we walk out this genuine tension between the principles of firstfruits and flow and our financial reality.

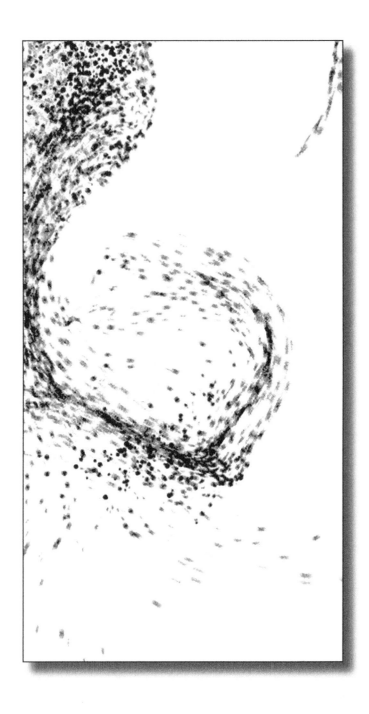

The Grace of Giving

But just as you excel in everything – in faith, in speech, in knowledge, in complete earnestness and in your love for us – see that you also excel in this grace of giving. (2 Corinthians 8:7)

C elebration filled the air as the worship band led the procession. The congregation sang and danced down the aisle of our small, picturesque, New England church. It was Giving Sunday! We were embarking on a major building project and the significant giving campaign that would accompany it. The congregation embraced the vision and the building plans that would house our growing family of ministries. People's minds and hearts were filled with excitement and anticipation, even knowing the daunting costs required for such an endeavor. We had secured some initial gifts, and now we were asking the congregation to add their generous contributions as well.

What we were undertaking was more than our growing, but still rather small, congregation could afford from the *extra* of our resources. So, we embarked on a two-month giving campaign in which we shared the vision the Lord was putting before us, the plans we had for the initial steps into that vision, and the invitation for the congregation to join with the ministry and with the Lord in this vision. As we shared, we specifically asked everyone to consider what he or she would give as an initial, firstfruits offering and then as a three-year commitment.

Our initial human response is always to ask ourselves, "What can I afford to give from my *overflow*?" Instead, we challenged the people to seek the Lord for what he wanted them to give. Then, through appropriate prayer, weighing, and testing with the Lord, they were to determine their financial commitment. The giving campaign culminated with Giving Sunday, when everyone would bring forward his or her firstfruits offering along with a three-year commitment card. At this point, the vision had been cast, the teaching was completed, and testimonies and encouraging stories had been shared. Now came the celebration as together we joyfully brought forward our God-directed offerings.

Lisa sat in the back row, her usual seat. She had exuberantly embraced the vision and held high expectations for Giving Sunday. Lisa had taken to heart the challenge set before her to seek the Lord first for how much she would give. She didn't have a lot of money, and what she did have was shared with her husband, who was not an active part of our church community. How could she possibly ask him to agree to an *extra* gift for a giving campaign? But as Lisa sought the Lord, she heard and saw in her mind's eye a distinct 1-3-0-0. She welled up with excitement and trepidation. Her spirit overflowed with joy at the prospect of giving $1300, but as the days and weeks marched toward Giving Sunday, $1300 seemed more and more impossible. There wasn't $1300 to start with, there wasn't any prospect she knew of that would bring her that kind of money, and there was no guarantee if they had $1300 she would be able to give it away. Yet Lisa knew what she heard and saw. She determinedly held onto the Lord's word and hoped for the miraculous.

Giving Sunday arrived, and Lisa's joy vanished, replaced with deep disappointment and a sense of failure. There definitely was no $1300, but there were a lot of unanswered questions. Had she let the Lord down since she could not bring what the Lord had told her to bring? Or had she not heard him correctly? How could she set herself up for failure with such an unrealistic expectation? In her demoralized state, Lisa still determined to come to church. This was her church family, and she had embraced this campaign; but there would be no celebration in her heart as she watched those around her joyfully experiencing the moment.

Lisa made one last consolation to the Lord. If she could not present $1300, she would empty her purse and give him all she had. It was all she could do. She scrounged around for what she could find and counted it out: $13.00 — the exact numbers the Lord had shown her two months before! She hadn't failed. The Lord knew exactly what she would be able to offer him — namely, all she had in her possession that Sunday morning. Lisa's deep disappointment turned to overflowing joy as she joined the procession down the aisle with her 1-3-0-0. It was all she had to offer, and it was exactly what the Lord was asking of her. He wasn't after $1300 but rather after Lisa's whole heart.

We often confuse what we have (and don't have) with our heart attitudes about what we will hold and cling to and what we will give away. We confuse poverty with a spirit of poverty and prosperity with a spirit of generosity. We call poverty the problem and prosperity the solution, while a spirit of poverty hovers just behind our consciousness, trying to gain control. We default to defining, and therefore measuring, generosity by quantity. In so doing we dismiss the spirit of generosity altogether, and it goes unfulfilled.

Let's examine the spirit of generosity and how it battles the spirit of poverty. Let's define and seek to understand how they shape our perspective and affect our approach to giving. What does the Lord require of us? What is the heart attitude he desires? Can we actually find freedom in the colliding realities of what we have, what we don't have, what we are invited to give, and how we are to feel about it? What does 2 Corinthians 8:7 mean by *excel in the grace of giving*?

Rich Generosity

Let's begin by looking at a story we find in the earliest days of the church. A devastating famine gripped the land of Israel. Caught in the center of it, in the city of Jerusalem, the early believers were experiencing double jeopardy. Struggling to survive the famine conditions, they also were enduring significant persecution for being part of the radical Christian movement. In his letter to the believers in Corinth, the apostle Paul used this occasion both to appeal for an offering for the desperate Jerusalem church and to instruct the Corinthians on the kingdom principles surrounding giving.

> *And now, brothers, we want you to know about the grace that God has given the Macedonian churches. Out of the most severe trial, their overflowing joy and their extreme poverty welled up in rich generosity. For I testify that they gave as much as they were able, and even beyond their ability. Entirely on their own, they urgently pleaded with us for the privilege of sharing in this service to the saints.* (2 Corinthians 8:1-4)

These few short verses are loaded with dramatic phrases: "most severe trial," "overflowing joy," "extreme poverty," "rich generosity," "beyond their ability," "urgently pleaded," and "privilege of sharing." This is not an "average day in the life." Rather, a vortex set of extreme conditions has overtaken average. Such occasions reveal core realities as they are squeezed to the surface and express themselves in our thoughts and actions. In this instance Paul referred to the story of how the Macedonian churches chose to respond to a particular situation, and he invited the church at Corinth to do the same.

The famine was not restricted to the land of Israel, as the impact was felt all over what is now known as the Middle East. Of course, some were suffering more from the famine than others, such as the Macedonians (just north of Corinth), who were in extreme poverty. As with the believers in Jerusalem, the economic conditions were compounded by persecution. Paul described it as severe trial. Yet in stark contrast, he also identified their overflowing joy, which was so great that these poor and persecuted believers gave with rich generosity. In fact, Paul said they gave not only what they were able but also beyond what they were able. How can that be? When you have nothing, how can you give? And even if you do give, how can you give *beyond* your ability? In order for this story and these polar opposite descriptors to make sense, we need to examine them more deeply. What assumptions are we making, and what deeper truths are actually being revealed in this passage of Scripture?

First, let's look at the phrase "rich generosity." Our default perspective assumes that in order to be richly generous we must be generously rich. We assume that generosity is measured in terms of "how much" we give. Therefore, *rich* generosity must mean "how much *more*" we give. Yet we see that the Macedonians did not have "how much more," but rather "how much *less*." The only descriptions are of how little they had. They were in poverty, in extreme poverty.

We think that to step into rich generosity, we must be able to give plentifully, which means we must have an overflow of resources from which to give. The more overflow we have, the more we can give, or overflow, to others. Often we even convince ourselves that the greater the overflow of our resources, the more joyfully we will give. But, in fact, the only thing the Macedonians were overflowing in was joy. They faced severe trials and extreme poverty but had overflowing joy. They mixed those three ingredients together and produced rich generosity. Joy proves to be the ingredient that alters the circumstances. Joy triumphed over trial and poverty, so much so that their rich generosity is described as giving *even beyond their ability*. Joy so stirred them that they *urgently pleaded* for the opportunity to give.

Measuring Generosity

To understand this Scripture further, we must shift our thinking from some default assumptions to truly kingdom principles. Most significantly, we must dispel the notion that generosity is measured in quantity. If we substitute quantity for generosity, the math simply does not work. Extreme poverty (meaning having nothing or less than nothing) multiplied by severe trial simply cannot result in a large quantity. But this passage should be no different than any other Scripture and scriptural principles that repeatedly challenge us to understand the central truth that God judges the heart. God always judges our hearts. Paul highlighted kingdom principles that supersede circumstances. Extreme poverty and severe trial were the circumstances, but the gospel had come to the Macedonians and, with it, joy overflowing. They had joy in receiving the gospel message itself, joy in the privilege of helping others in need, and joy in the unquestioning confidence that the Lord would take care of them through his love and provision. So there was joy, and it naturally overflowed. Poverty is real and measurable. Trials are real and to a certain extent measurable. I'm not sure how we measure joy, yet it is so powerfully real that it actually overshadows the two measurable realities of poverty and trials.

Consider these three components: poverty, trial, and joy. We can define and measure poverty because its source is external and finite. We derive money and resources from external and measurable means. Trials also are external and therefore definable and measurable. By contrast, the joy in this story is immeasurable because of its source. It overflowed from the infinite reservoir of the presence of the Holy Spirit (infinite as long as the people remained tapped into that source). Paul plainly identified this set of circumstances that defied measurement. Therefore, the resulting *rich generosity* could not be measured either. The external and measurable components (poverty, trials) were overwhelmed by the immeasurable, internal flow of joy, and so the result was also an immeasurable expression of generosity. Rich generosity described the Macedonians' hearts, not the amount of their gift.

Since we can measure poverty and trials but not joy that flows from the heart, then why do we tend to put generosity in the category of the former, which is measurable? This story shows us that generosity is not a measurable quantity. In fact, the immeasurable but overriding dynamic of joy has a greater influence on generosity than do the very real presence of poverty and trials. The Macedonians gave with rich generosity, not with a meager amount or meager expression of generosity. While the actual financial gift may have been meager, Paul made no reference to the amount. He simply described their gift the same way he described their joyful hearts.

Poverty, Prosperity, a Spirit of Poverty, and a Spirit of Generosity

To further understand these distinctions, let's contrast poverty with a spirit of poverty and prosperity with a spirit of generosity. By definition poverty is *not having*. A spirit of poverty, by contrast, is the *fear of not having* or the *fear of losing* what you do have. Poverty describes our external circumstances. We either have, or we don't have. However, a spirit of poverty is a heart attitude about those external circumstances. When we make this distinction, it is easy to see how completely and even significantly different poverty is from a spirit of poverty.

With this distinction, we also can easily identify each of them. Poverty stares at us. Whether we've experienced it, seen it, or simply know of it, we don't have any difficulty identifying poverty. However, it is also easy to identify a spirit of poverty, or the fear of not having. We know what that fear feels like. Most of us have seen or even experienced this spirit ourselves. In fact, we may even know people who have significant wealth and yet operate with a spirit of poverty. They have a nagging fear of losing what they have. They constantly doubt the sufficiency of what they have. They live and act as if they were poor; excessively guarding what they have, stingy in how they use it, and constantly concerned about their provision. This spirit forces them to cling to what they have and worry about what they don't have. A spirit of poverty can wrap its ugly tentacles around a person's spirit and even restrict life itself.

The same distinction exists between prosperity and a spirit of generosity. Prosperity is the external, measurable reality and circumstance of *having*. A spirit of generosity is not at all limited by the external amount of what we have (or equally, by what we don't have). A spirit of generosity is the heart attitude that desires to share and bless others through giving.

A spirit of poverty has a central concern for oneself. It says, "I need to have, and I need to make sure that I will always have." By contrast, a spirit of generosity has a central concern for others: "I want them to have." We can also distinguish a spirit of generosity from giving itself. Giving can be motivated by many different things, not only by a spirit of generosity. We can give out of obligation, out of the desire to get something in return, or even out of guilt. In addition, we can give wonderfully from the overflow of what we have, and we're often encouraged to do so. This is good, but giving a measured amount from the measured overflow of what we have is better described as philanthropy. A spirit of generosity is an internal heart desire to bless others out of concern for them. It is not measured by what we have but flows from the desire of our hearts. In Paul's description in 2 Corinthians 8, the only component of the Macedonians' situation that was overflowing was joy. The only component that reflected their heart attitude was the very component that qualified the gift as *rich* — the overflowing joy that led to rich generosity.

Jesus provided this same commentary about an incident he witnessed in the temple. He took the opportunity to teach his disciples these same principles in a sliver of Scripture recorded by both Luke and Mark.

> *As he looked up, Jesus saw the rich putting their gifts into the temple treasury. He also saw a poor widow put in two very small copper coins. "I tell you the truth," he said, "this poor widow has put in more than all the others. All these people gave their gifts out of their wealth; but she out of her poverty put in all she had to live on."* (Luke 21:1-4)

Jesus made it clear that his measure was not quantity, for he declared that the impoverished woman put in *more* than all the others. He pointed out that she gave out of her poverty, just as the Macedonians, who gave out of extreme poverty. Jesus added that the woman in fact gave all she had. Again, this parallels the Macedonians, who gave even beyond what they were able. All the others, Jesus said, gave out of their wealth. The Greek word used for *wealth* in Luke 21:4 actually means "to exceed a fixed number of measure, to be left over and above a certain number or measure." In other words, Jesus was saying the others were giving out of their extra or overflow. In contrast, the woman did not give for show. She did not give the extra that she had because there was no extra. In fact, there was not even enough. Jesus pointed out to his disciples that she may have been impoverished but she refused to be defined by a spirit of poverty.

The Grace of Giving

We live in a fallen world, and it's sad that many who love the Lord will die in abject poverty. It is also true that many will reject the love of the Lord and the truth of his gospel and yet flourish in this world, at least financially. The fall of mankind ushered in poverty and inequality. Some may have the opportunity to change their circumstances and rise out of the ashes of poverty. Many will never have that chance. Yet everyone can choose to rise above a spirit of poverty and embrace the spirit of generosity.

The Lord desires us to find our sufficiency in him, to have the confidence that he is our provision, to be so transformed by the reality that we overflow with joy, and then for the overflowing joy to result in overflowing generosity. So true, so real, so transformational was the presence of the gospel in the Macedonians' spirits that they *urgently pleaded* for the opportunity to overflow their joy through an expression of rich generosity.

Lisa brought her $13.00 to the altar that Giving Sunday. It was a richly generous gift birthed in a joyful heart that desperately wanted to overflow and be a blessing to others. We measure what we know how to measure: our circumstances, our resources, what we have and what we don't have. Often we do not control how much we have. One of the results of living in this fallen world is a regular struggle for provision and, for many, even poverty. One of the results of breaking our relationship with our heavenly Father through the fall is that heart attitudes, which were intended to be God-focused, are instead dominated by self-centered perspectives. As we restore the relationship with our heavenly Father, we find the ability to put our trust in his provision.

> *So do not worry, saying, "What shall we eat?" or "What shall we drink"' or "What shall we wear?" For the pagans run after all these things, and your heavenly Father knows that you need them. But seek first his kingdom and his righteousness, and all these things will be given to you as well.* (Matthew 6:31-33)

We may not always be financially comfortable or have confidence about what we will need for tomorrow. However, the Lord's invitation is to put our confidence in him today. When we are able to depend on his provision (and trust his love and his desire to be our provider), then we must reject the spirit of poverty that wants to dominate us. The truth of the gospel and our confidence in the Lord needs to result in godly heart attitudes, including overflowing joy and a spirit of generosity.

The apostle Paul was determined to bring clarity to this understanding as he continued his instruction to the Corinthians. He wrote, *"I am not commanding you, but I want to test the sincerity of your love"* (2 Corinthians 8:8). A gift given in response to a command would be measured and externally motivated. Paul made it clear that the best gift is that which comes from the heart. It must flow from love and a desire to bless others. Paul continued, *"For if the willingness is there, the gift is acceptable according to what one has, not according to what he does not have"* (2 Corinthians 8:12). Paul invited the Corinthians to join the Macedonian churches in having hearts of compassion, love, and a desire to bless others out of overflowing joy. The gift is not measured by the amount. The measure is simply the willingness and desire to give.

Paul summarized his teaching with this charge to the Corinthians: *"But just as you excel in everything – in faith, in speech, in knowledge, in complete earnestness and in your love for us – see that you also excel in this grace of giving"* (2 Corinthians 8:7). Giving is a grace. We should pursue it as we do faith, love, and all other graces. Giving is an external act, but it is not meant to be calculated and measured. It's a response to an internal overflow of love, compassion, and joy. The external, dramatic circumstances facing the Macedonian church definitely affected the amount they could give, but they didn't limit the flow of grace. Severe trial, overflowing joy, and extreme poverty resulted in rich generosity. How was that possible? It was possible because the Macedonian believers excelled in grace, the grace of giving.

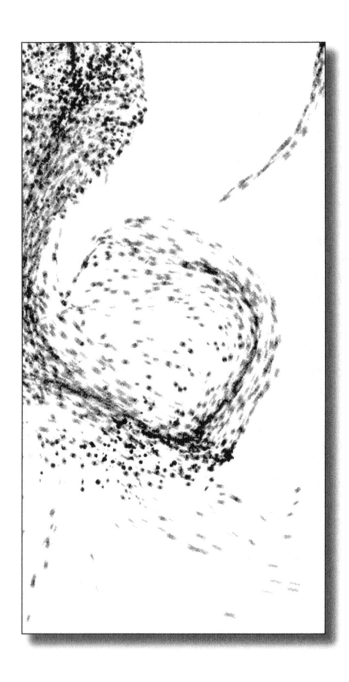

A Lifestyle of Generosity

Give, and it will be given to you. A good measure,
pressed down, shaken together and running over,
will be poured into your lap. For with the measure
you use, it will be measured to you. (Luke 6:38)

I reached into my pocket and realized all I had was a
fifty-cent coin. Should I, or shouldn't I? The offering
plate was coming quickly, and I had to decide now. Do
I give everything in my pocket or nothing? I had no
third option. It had to be all or nothing, and I had to
decide now.

As a young teen I was attending a monthly regional
youth rally. Bible quiz teams would compete as part of
the night's program. Our church's team was scheduled
for this month so we were sitting in the front pew.
After a welcome and some songs, they called for an

offering. That's when I reached into my pocket and found that the only coin I had was a fifty-cent piece. I don't know why I had the coin. Even when they used to mint fifty-cent pieces, it was not a common coin. However, on that particular Friday night, one of these coins occupied my pocket—all by itself. The offering plates were first passed to the front row. Just as in every church I had ever seen, the plates would start at the front and work their way back. I had no time to contemplate my options. My hand inside my pocket firmly held this coin of decision.

I was raised to understand and practice tithing. Beginning with a dime allowance, I would place a penny in the offering. I continued to faithfully tithe as the allowances increased or I acquired pocket money earned from any odd job I could find. Even the week of this youth rally, I'm sure I had maintained my practice and given my tithe in my own church. This fifty cents would be above and beyond, and it was all that I had. For me, in those days and in my situation, it was a meaningful amount. I can actually recall thinking, "I wish I could give only some of this amount or somehow make change." I really did not want to give all I had in my pocket, but I knew there was no other option, and within seconds the decision had to be made. I pulled my hand out of my pocket and placed the coin in the offering plate. I could not change my decision. Yet I distinctly remember continuing to question my decision, even though there was no reversing it.

Next, a guest speaker was invited to the pulpit. Beginning with an illustration, he stepped down from the platform and singled me out for his illustration partner. Of all things, the little demonstration centered around a one-dollar bill that passed back and forth between his hand and mine. It ended with me holding the dollar bill. As he turned to return to the pulpit, I extended my arm to hand him back his dollar. He nearly ignored me, giving me a quick wave behind himself, indicating for me to keep it. Amazed, I looked around, but no one else was privy to my God moment. I sat back down, my mind grappling with what had just happened.

I don't really remember the speaker's illustration, and I definitely don't remember what he talked about. Thoughts preoccupied my head. Emotions rolled through my soul. At that time, at that age, and at my level of experience, I did not have the spiritual language to articulate what had just happened. However, I gained a spiritual truth that was as clear as any experience I could possibly have. Without a doubt, I knew then and I know now what the Lord was saying to me. If I would choose to open my hands and not cling to protect what I had, if I would generously give what I had (and what I have), I would always find him to be faithful and my source of provision and blessing.

It was only fifty cents. It was only one coin. I could share with you many other stories with much bigger dollar signs. I could share about times when I was working in the corporate world. I could tell about the time I received an unexpected bonus, and my wife and I knew it was not for us since we had been inspired by the vision of another ministry that was in financial need. I could relate the time when we took my raise and offered it for a full year as firstfruits for things to come or times when both my wife and I made decisions about jobs and careers. Yet I chose to share my boyhood story because through it the Lord introduced me to this principle in a way that has shaped my life ever since. The dollar amounts may get bigger and the decisions may seem weightier, but the principles are the same. The fact that I can recall my experience from forty years ago with such detail and clarity confirms to me that it was a moment with God. When I recall the story, I don't merely remember the facts; I also feel the emotions, the experience, all over again. It does not feel like it happened just yesterday, but it is a vivid recollection, and it is something I treasure. What the Lord taught me has never stopped speaking to me. My confidence is this: As I live generously before the Lord and choose to maintain a posture of open hands and not cling to what I have, my God will be ever and always faithful to provide for me and bless me. In the freedom of knowing that God will fully sustain me, I pursue a lifestyle of generosity.

And God Is Able (2 Corinthians 9:6-12)

It is for freedom that Christ has set us free. Experiencing freedom in the area of finances, with a spirit of generosity and a desire to bless others, is a real challenge for many of us. We would like to bless others more. We would like to be more generous. We would like to experience a greater sense of freedom, but we get entangled. We would like to joyfully give more, but that seems impossible because of our situations. Honest thoughts that run through our minds may sound like these.

- I want to give generously, but I know that means I will have less to meet *my* real needs.
- I know I'm supposed to give (or should give) to this need or worthwhile situation, so I'll give even though my spirit and mind are reluctant.
- I will give but only sparingly so that I will still be okay.

- I know I can't afford to, but I'll at least give something because I'm obligated.

These struggles and the underlying mindsets are addressed in a short instructional passage of Scripture. The joy of giving, the joy of being generous, the stranglehold of frugality, the fullness of God's provision, the ability to be a blessing, the opportunity to glorify God through helping others, and the freedom that comes with the confidence of God's faithfulness—the apostle Paul addressed all these principles in his second letter to the church at Corinth. We have previously looked at the example he shared with the Corinthian church concerning the Macedonian believers and their spiritual gift of giving (2 Corinthians 8). In chapter 9 Paul continued by laying out the foundational principles for a lifestyle of generosity. Let's take an in-depth look at this passage so that we can begin to experience a generous lifestyle of our own.

"And God is able to make all grace abound to you, so that in all things at all times, having all that you need, you will abound in every good work" (2 Corinthians 9:8). This is a bold and grand statement. By using superlatives, Paul seems to place this declaration outside the realm of our normal experience: *all* grace, *all* things, *all* times, *all* that you need, *every* good work. This is simply an over-the-top declaration. We want to say, "Come on, Paul; get real. This may happen to some people all the time and all people some of the time, but not to all of us all the time. Stop exaggerating." We may even wish it weren't in the Scriptures, because now we need to believe it. Our faith in the Bible obligates us to believe it, but our experience refutes what is being declared. What should we do with this passage? Do we believe in spite of what we know, or do we know better?

What is truly being said here? What principles and foundational truths was Paul declaring?

To answer that question, let's begin with the opening phrase: *"and God is able."* We must take a critical look at this opening declaration; otherwise, everything that follows makes no sense and has no foundation. These opening four words contain two very important and distinct declarations. To say that God *is* able is not the same as saying that God always does or always will do everything that follows. The declaration is that God is able to completely accomplish everything expressed in the rest of the verse. God is not whimsical, and there is no uncertainty to his will or character; but we need to recognize that this is a conditional statement. God *is* able. The second declaration in this opening phrase is that "God is *able*" to accomplish all that this verse promises. In fact, the Greek word translated "able" has a stronger meaning than the English understanding of the word. It means to be powerful or mighty. God is powerful enough and mighty enough to bring forth the fulfillment of all the superlative declarations that follow.

What is God able to do? He is able to *"make all grace abound to you."* We read this verse, and we naturally apply it to the realm of finances. Although I believe these principles apply broadly as general foundational truths, it's true that Paul here specifically was addressing a financial situation with the church at Corinth. Therefore, it is appropriate to apply this instruction to our understanding of giving and finances. It's noteworthy, then, that Paul declared God's ability to make all *grace* abound to us. He did not say God will make our financial resources an overflowing bounty. He specifically was talking about a financial situation throughout this teaching, yet he clearly made the distinction that the grace of the Lord will abound (also translated, "overflow") to us.

In its simplest definition, grace is receiving what we don't deserve. It is a gift. We don't merit or justify receiving it. It comes from the goodwill, intent, and choice of the giver. God graces us. Included in his overflowing grace can be financial means, but grace is so much more. It is the Lord's presence, the Lord's wisdom, the Lord's peace, divinely orchestrated connections, divinely fitted circumstances, and more. God's grace to us should result in and be reflected in our faith and trust in the Lord. We are inspired to praise and worship. Our love for and confidence in our Lord increases, as well as our passion for a deeper relationship and a pursuit of his incomprehensible, abounding grace.

Abounding Grace

"And God is able to make all grace abound to you, so that in all things at all times, having all that you need..." In abounding grace we lack nothing. God's grace is not a measured grace. It's an abounding grace. It's an overflowing amount of grace. The word translated "abound" means to exceed in measure, even to an immeasurable amount. God's grace is not limited, and it will be more than enough for all things at all times.

It's important that we understand the phrase, *"having all that you need."* Also translated "enough," it can be defined as a perfect condition of life in which no aid or support is needed, a sufficiency of the necessities of life, or a mind contented with its lot, that is, contentment. *Having all that you need* is categorically different and abundantly more than simply having your financial needs met. We can actually have financial stability and yet not feel the contentment and sense of sufficiency that is spoken of here. Abounding grace accomplishes significantly more than providing financial stability. Abounding grace brings sufficiency to our lives and contentment to our minds. As we understand and embrace God's overflowing grace available to us, we discover the larger truths of this verse (all things, at all times, all we need) easily contained in his abounding grace.

What a wonderful gift and absolute blessing this is! Yet, astonishingly, the end purpose for this abounding grace is not simply to personally receive it but rather to lead to abounding good works: *"And God is able to make all grace abound to you, so that... you will abound in every good work."* The superlatives (all things, at all times, all we need) are part of the *flow* of grace, not its end purpose. The value of God's grace far exceeds its direct blessing to us. Grace abounds. Grace is immeasurable. It can't be measured by simply meeting our needs. When God's grace flows, it knows no bounds. We cannot use it up or consume all of it ourselves. It flows to *every good work* that we give ourselves to. In fact, it *abounds* in every good work. God desires to release his abounding grace to us so that it may boundlessly flow through us. What a comprehensively powerful verse this is. God has the ability, the power and might, to overflow us with endless grace. His abundant grace will bring contentment to our whole lives and sufficiently supply all our needs. And the result (and purpose) will be a limitless flow of good works on behalf of others.

Sowing and Reaping

God is able. He has the ability, the power and might, to bring forth an endless release of grace. This is true, but as we stated earlier, this is a conditional declaration. So what is or what are the conditions that allow us to experience this release of God's grace? To answer that question, let's look back two verses and see what Paul was presenting to the Corinthians.

Whoever sows sparingly will also reap sparingly, and whoever sows generously will also reap generously. Each man should give what he has decided in his heart to give, not reluctantly or under compulsion, for God loves a cheerful giver. (2 Corinthians 9:6-7)

As Paul was asking the Corinthians to prepare their special offering to support the persecuted and drought-inflicted Christians in Jerusalem, he gave them this straightforward instruction. If you sow sparingly, then the return on that investment will be just as small. The original Greek word translated "sparingly" also can be translated "stingily." If we sow sparingly, we are being stingy because from our perspective, calculation, or desire it's all we can or are willing to spare. However, when we pour out our gifts generously, we will reap a great harvest.

The principle of sowing and reaping sounds like common sense. If we look at Paul's instruction by itself, we can easily apply this proverb to nearly all circumstances or areas of life. We get out of something what we put into it. This is standard motivational instruction for any coach, trainer, teacher, mentor, parent, employer, etc. If one wants to be a good athlete, he or she must train. A musician can't even count the voluminous number of hours that has gone into perfecting his or her craft. We expect doctors to have studied and trained to perfection. So, on the one hand, this statement by Paul is nothing more than a repeat of common sense or common wisdom. The power and the hook in what Paul wrote lies in the situation to which he was applying this proverb. He was instructing the Corinthians regarding giving away what they had. In the natural, this investment has no return. In the natural, the opposite of sowing and reaping would seem to apply. It would seem that the less we give away, the more we will retain for ourselves. Likewise, the more generous we are, the less we will have for ourselves. So Paul's instruction was no simple, commonsense wisdom. It was radically different. He was instructing the Corinthians to view this special collection from a different perspective. Instead of considering what they would normally view as the end of the matter, Paul challenged them to view as only the beginning. We (like the Corinthians) normally think that when we give, whether it is a little or a lot, it is gone. Even if we see the value in blessing others, we still view our gift as a one-way transaction that ends at the moment we give. Whatever we give we no longer have. In contrast, Paul taught that there is a return on the gift, and it will be directly proportional to the amount given.

Let's be clear, this verse also has been taken as a stand-alone principle and too often misused to defend the "prosperity gospel." This teaching asserts that God directly rewards people in proportion and in kind for their offerings to him (or to the church presenting this teaching). In a proper reading of Scripture, this verse does not stand alone. It appears in context and in conjunction with further teaching and understanding. Let's not start and stop with this verse. Let's not reduce a phenomenal principle of God's kingdom economy to a controlling give-and-take with the Lord. It's not for us to reduce God to some cosmic banker we can manipulate by how much we invest in his bank. Whoever sows sparingly also will reap sparingly, and whoever sows generously will reap generously. This is simple and easily understood, but what is the rest of the teaching?

Giving Cheerfully

Along with the principle of sowing and reaping, Paul addressed the matter of having the right heart, or spiritual, attitude about giving. He wrote, *"Each man should give what he has decided in his heart to give, not reluctantly or under compulsion, for God loves a cheerful giver"* (2 Corinthians 9:7). We are to give what we have decided in our heart to give. As we give to bless others, our heart in the matter is as important as the gift itself. In fact, we are instructed not to give out of compulsion or even reluctantly. God's desire is for us to give from a cheerful heart. Anything else detracts from the spiritual principle of sowing and reaping. If this were simply a monetary transaction, this would not be true. However, the Lord's desire is for us to reap generously, not simply in finances but in a much more comprehensive way, as we reap abounding grace. Giving reluctantly is not giving with the spirit or the grace the Lord desires. Giving cheerfully and desiring to bless others comes from a heart that aligns with God's heart. Therefore, it will have great impact and a great return, an abounding return.

If we are to abound in God's grace, seeing his abounding grace flow through us to others, we must have the same heart that beats within him. His heart is always concerned with all his children, every one of whom he loves. We are called to have the same heart and attitude that Christ had, which was not to be concerned about himself but to give himself for the sake of others. In his case, Jesus actually gave up his throne in heaven and went to the cross for those he and his heavenly Father loved (Philippians 2:4-8). When we give sparingly because we are concerned about our own well-being, or reluctantly, or from a sense of obligation, our gift does not carry the heart of Christ in it. When our desire is to bless others and we generously give from what we have out of a concern for others, we tap into the heartbeat of the Father and his abounding grace.

We need to clearly state again that generosity is not measured by quantity. We've distinguished between prosperity, generosity, and a spirit of generosity. God knows what we have, and he knows our hearts. He always desires to first have our hearts aligned with his. Then, with our hearts in right alignment, we will be generous givers regardless of our circumstances (spirit of generosity). If we have wayward hearts or hardened hearts, we will give sparingly and from the wrong spirit, even if the quantity may be significant. Sure, the money may be useful in the moment, but the principle of sowing and reaping will still apply. Our gift will yield a sparse return. Freedom is found in knowing that the Lord delights in each and every heart that beats with concern and compassion for the same things and in the same way as his heart.

"God is able." And to whom is God able to make grace abound so that it overflows with all that we need, at all times, and for all things, allowing us to abound in every good work? It's to those who sow generously. It's to those who give with a cheerful heart. They have aligned their hearts with the Lord's heart and opened a channel for grace to flow. When grace flows, it knows no bounds. It will abound to the generous,

cheerful-hearted giver, and it will flow through and to others in their good works. This will continue as long as there is generous sowing from cheerful hearts, and it will continue as long as there is an open flow of good works to others.

If we pinch off the flow by not sowing generously or with a cheerful heart, the channel of grace will dry up. If we stop the flow by not extending ourselves in good works to others, the flow of grace also will end. However, to all who generously sow and cheerfully give, God will make all grace abound, and it will be more than enough for us and for the godly work of our hands. A lifestyle of generosity encompasses much more than the amount of our giving. It's a lifestyle of overflowing, cheerful hearts aligned with God's heart and his compassionate desire to bless others. It's a lifestyle that understands and embraces the practice of sowing generously, and it opens a flow of abundant grace to and through us. It's a lifestyle that not only receives a flow of grace but also lives in its sufficiency in full contentment and through good works extends that grace to others. A gift is a good and sometimes God-directed blessing to others. A generous gift is a big blessing. A lifestyle of generosity is a lifestyle that demonstrates that we understand and experience the reality of the truth that *God is able*.

In verse 9 Paul punctuated this principle and profound truth by taking it even further — indeed, into eternity. Not only does grace abound in a generous lifestyle, but it also actually reveals a righteousness that will endure forever. Paul stated, *"As it is written: 'He has scattered abroad his gifts to the poor; his righteousness endures forever'"* (2 Corinthians 9:9). Quoting from Psalm 112, Paul showed that when we freely extend ourselves to the poor through gifts of generosity, we are performing an act of eternal righteousness (right-living in alignment with God). Paul invited the Corinthian believers to enter into the special offering for the desperate needs of the believers in Jerusalem. Through a gift that was birthed from a generous spirit, they would experience abounding grace and righteousness that would also endure forever.

A Harvest of Righteousness

After establishing the foundational understanding of a generous lifestyle, Paul turned his attention to the outworking of such a lifestyle, writing, *"Now he who supplies seed to the sower and bread for food will also supply and increase your store of seed and will enlarge the harvest of your righteousness"* (2 Corinthians 9:10). It is God who supplies *"seed to the sower"* and *"bread for food."* This is the abundant grace we have been talking about. Seed is for planting. In the imagery of this chapter, the seed is our gifts to the poor and those in need. *"Bread for food"* is the Lord's faithfulness to provide all that we need at all times for all things. The verse not only speaks to God's ability and promise to supply seed for sowing and bread for food, but even more, it declares increase and enlargement. This part is easy to embrace, isn't it? We all would like to see increase and enlargement in the area of finances, and this verse declares that God, who supplies the seed and the bread, also will bring an increase and an enlargement. But look closely at the verse again. What will the Lord increase? He will increase the store of seed. Seed is what we sow; therefore *"your store of seed"* is the ability through abounding, overflowing grace to be able to sow even more.

Whoever sows sparingly will also reap sparingly, and whoever sows generously will also reap generously.

As we sow generously, the Lord supplies and increases our *store of seed*. One of the things we will generously reap is an increased ability and capability to sow. This may mean we will have increased opportunities to sow. It may mean we will have additional resources to sow. It may mean we will have an increase in our compassion and desire to bless others no matter what the cost. The God who supplies the seed will increase the store of seed, opening a flow of generosity that will never dry up. If our hearts are cheerful and aligned with God, and if our desire is to bless others, and if our sowing is with a full spirit of generosity, the store of seed will never be depleted, and the flow will continue in abundant good works. We may desire an increase in our finances, but this principle of God's kingdom economy centers on the flow from a generous lifestyle, a flow that will increase our storehouse of seed for more sowing.

Verse 10 also states that along with increasing our store of seed, the Lord will enlarge our harvest. Again, we would all delight in any enlargement of the bread for food the Lord provides. Indeed, we can always enlarge what we need to maintain our lives, the harvest of our labor. Yet Paul stated that as we live a lifestyle of generosity, God will enlarge our *harvest of righteousness*. The increase is more seed for sowing. The enlargement is a greater harvest of righteousness. The blessing of a lifestyle of generosity is a growing harvest of righteousness. Again, righteousness is simply understood as right living in alignment with God. His kingdom economy bears fruit that has value in his kingdom: a store of seed (the ability to continue to give generously), and a harvest of righteousness (the blessing of a closer and purer relationship with our heavenly Father). The Bible calls this "fruit that will last" (John 15:16).

Paul continued, *"You will be made rich in every way so that you can be generous on every occasion, and through us your generosity will result in thanksgiving to God"* (2 Corinthians 9:11). We cannot contain or measure the richness of a generous lifestyle. With a cheerful heart, a desire to bless, and a passion for others, the generous spirit overflows by the abounding grace of God. A lifestyle of generosity seeks every occasion to be generous. And beyond all that, it results *"in thanksgiving to God."* Not only will we be helping others and not only will we be actively ministering God's kingdom of love and hope, but we will also see thankful hearts thanking God. In fact, the remaining verses of this chapter continue to express all the ways people will give thanks to God. They will see the spirit of generosity helping others and will thank God for it. They will see the obedience of those who profess the gospel and will thank God for it. Abounding grace and a spirit of generosity are an open flow of God's life and love through us to others. As we express God's kingdom and his heart, those who witness this grace and generosity will not only be thankful for what they receive, but they will also praise God for the blessings of his kingdom. They may not fully understand or use that language, but they will be touched by the good news of the kingdom, and they will praise God.

Paul summed up this whole perspective and understanding by calling it, *"the surpassing grace God has given you"* (2 Corinthians 9:14). We have the opportunity to live a lifestyle of generosity, sowing generously with cheerful hearts, not reluctantly or out of compulsion. We have the opportunity to reap a generous reward of abundant grace that is not only sufficient for all of our needs at all times but also allows us to abound in good works. As we live this lifestyle, we will find the Lord increasing our ability to be generous and drawing us into ever-greater levels of righteousness. And through it all, the flow of surpassing grace and generosity will result in praise to our God.

The Fifty-cent Piece, Part 2

I began this chapter by sharing my boyhood experience with the fifty-cent piece. What the Lord awakened in me then, I have now experienced for a lifetime. I bear witness to the truth that a willing heart of generosity releases a flow of grace that is more than sufficient for us, blesses others, and brings praise to our God. A few years ago at the church I pastor, we found ourselves in a financial crisis. We were led to believe that our finances were being managed well and that we were financially stable. We were not, and by the mercy of the Lord, he revealed it to us before it was too late. We took a number of immediate actions necessary to put us back on a course of integrity and good stewardship and headed us toward stability. It proved to be a most difficult season but one that revealed God's faithfulness once again.

A month after we became aware of the crisis and began taking the necessary steps in response, I was walking down the hallway in the church on a Sunday morning between services. As I passed the church office, I saw a penny on the floor. Picking it up I decided I would put it in the offering. Behind me on the wall of the church office is a mail slot, where our ushers place the offerings after they have been collected. I turned around with the penny in hand, smiling to myself about the silliness of adding a penny to the offering in a time of such need. As I placed the penny through the mail slot, I heard the Lord say in my spirit, "Give your fifty-cent piece also."

A few months prior I had turned fifty years old. A friend of mine who is also the prayer deacon of our church had given me a birthday card with a fifty-cent coin in it. She knew nothing of my boyhood encounter. She was simply giving me a cute birthday card and gift since we had joked with each other about entering the fifty-year-old club. At the time I was not aware of the crisis we were entering, but I did know our finances were not as sound as they should be; so I decided to carry the coin in my pocket as a reminder of my confidence and trust in the grace of the Lord, the confidence I had walked in my whole life. I carried the coin around for three months. I lost it a couple of times in the couch cushions, where we had to dig around to retrieve it. I even toted it on a mission trip to Uganda and back. Every time I put my hand in my pocket, I could feel God's faithful provision. It had expanded from a personal symbol to now include the ministry I was charged with leading.

So there I stood in church on a Sunday morning with the Lord prompting me to place the fifty-cent piece in the mail slot—in the offering again! I am amazed how our minds, spirits, and emotions work. Immediately I was thirteen again, and I did not want to place the coin in the slot. I thought, "No! This is my testimony of your faithfulness. This represents my witness." I was growing attached to the coin in my pocket and all it represented, but the argument in my mind lasted only a second. I reached into my pocket and for the second time in my life pulled out a fifty-cent coin and placed it into the offering. The weeks and months that followed were very difficult, but his grace abounds, and our church is again experiencing the flow of generosity and good works. Praise be to God for his faithfulness!

The Lord knew exactly how to demonstrate to me that my hope and confidence are in him and that should never change. My boyhood experience now had a powerful new chapter. The Lord is the same yesterday, today, and forever. My confidence remains steadfast. As I live generously before the Lord, and as I choose to maintain a posture of open hands and not cling to what I have, my God will be ever and always faithful to provide for and bless me. In the freedom of knowing that God will fully sustain me, I continue to pursue a lifestyle of generosity.

Giving to Vision

I am amply supplied, now that I have received from Epaphroditus the gifts you sent. They are a fragrant offering, an acceptable sacrifice, pleasing to God. And my God will meet all your needs according to his glorious riches in Christ Jesus. (Philippians 4:18-19)

On December 26, 2004, a tsunami roared through the Indian Ocean releasing unprecedented devastation. Three months later I traveled with a medical team to Southeast India. The trip had been planned prior to the tsunami, and our work would not be along the destroyed coastline; but we did have the opportunity to visit a village and see the destruction firsthand. The tent city painted the hillside behind the remains of rubble and debris. The sight stole our voices, as we stood silent before the scene. But we were also shocked by the mountains of donated clothes that had poured in from all over the world, already rotting in the humid heat of Southeast Asia. Compassionate and well-intentioned giving was not enough to provide the intended assistance. In this case, the infrastructure simply did not exist to complete the distribution.

In the midst of the chaos and overwhelming needs, the Indian ministry hosting our missions team had a vision. They conceived a plan to address the distribution issue as well as begin to rebuild both the villages and the people's lives. The ministry began to warehouse some of the outpouring of food and clothing at their facility. They adopted seven tsunami-ravaged villages within an hour's drive and set up a store in each. Every day trucks and vans traveled to each village to restock the stores, where the villagers could purchase what they needed. The currency? Vouchers, which they earned as they worked to rebuild their own village, even their own houses and fishing nets. So successful was this strategy that the elders of the villages began seeking advice and counsel from the ministry leaders for all aspects of their rebuilding and governing efforts. These Hindu elders even invited the ministry to start churches in the villages. For the people of these seven villages, the compassionate outpouring of help actually affected their lives.

Chasing Needs

How do we distinguish between heartfelt giving (which may or may not actually help) and contributing to needs or efforts that will make a difference? I am privileged to have a strong and wonderful ministry partnership and personal friendship with Bishop

Arnold Muwonge, a godly, wise man and successful ministry leader. As a Ugandan, he adds a healthy alternative perspective to my Western worldview. One thing he has observed as he has hosted many people from developed nations in his native Uganda is that visitors are suddenly gripped by what they witness in developing nations. The depth of need enwraps their hearts, and their minds are quickly spinning with plans and ideas. Bishop Muwonge has seen many attempts by compassionate, well-intentioned people trying to tackle the needs and solve the overwhelming problems of the people to whom they have just been exposed. In response he shares this wise instruction: "You can't chase needs. You must follow vision."

Before we continue our study of kingdom economic principles, let's discuss some practical parameters for giving as well. There are indeed many needs, and even atrocities, throughout the world that we, the believers in Christ, should be actively and passionately addressing. God cares about everyone and every need. Having compassion for those we see and choosing to bless them is always in line with God's heart. Simple acts of generosity or impulse gifts that are expressions of love and blessing are wonderful and should be encouraged. However, the perspective that we "can't chase needs" but "must follow vision" actually elevates this same compassionate motivation to a strategic and God-directed level. If we are the body of Christ, the practical hands and feet of his continued kingdom ministry to this world, we also must have the heartbeat of the Holy Spirit within us and the mind of Christ directing us.

If we do not align our efforts to help with the heart and vision of the Lord's direction for us, the needs of the world will overwhelm us. Simply giving ourselves and our resources to any and every need or ministry opportunity or request is not embracing the kingdom strategy of the Lord. Even Jesus said there will always be needs and the needy (John 12:8). Effective ministry and compassion that brings significant change must align with the Lord's intentions. It is then we also will fully activate and release the principles of God's kingdom's economy.

Consider all the variables that may wrap around any particular need we encounter. Is this a need our resources will actually help, or will attempting to help only delay addressing the real issue? Are there deeper problems that are causing this need to be a bottomless pit? Jesus himself instructed us not to cast pearls before swine (Matthew 7:6). We are not called to be blindly generous, and therefore careless, with what we have. Even when we are presented with a legitimate need, we should ask ourselves whether the Lord is directing *us* to give to this situation. It may very well be that the Lord is addressing this need in a different way or through a different person, while there are other specific things to which he would have us give. When we chase needs, we limit our ability (money, focus, compassion) to strategically follow vision, even the Lord's vision for us.

The complexities of a situation are not fully known except to the mind of Christ. Yet with the mind of Christ our gifts, generosity, and compassion can produce eternal significance. There are needs all around us. The strategic direction of the Lord as we follow vision invites us to open a channel for the flow of heaven's resources into a particular need, bringing his kingdom to earth. It's not our generous gifts that will ultimately meet the needs around us but that heavenly flow. The challenge for us is to operate in the economic principles of God's kingdom (flow, giving, generosity) as we are led by his vision and purpose.

Following Vision

Consider this principle, as we see it applied in the Bible. Jesus himself left a crowd of people who were seeking his hope and healing because he was directed by the Father to move on to another village (Matthew 8:18). Needs existed in both places, but one had a kingdom purpose. Jesus listened and obeyed the Father. He didn't chase need; rather, he followed vision and the direction of the Father. Years later, the apostle Paul prepared to travel to Bithynia to minister there but was prevented from doing so by the Holy Spirit. Instead, the Lord sent him in the opposite direction to Macedonia (Acts 16:6-10). The account of the story does not deny the real needs in both cities. The Holy Spirit redirected Paul and his team for a strategic purpose.

As we open our hearts and hands for generosity to flow, we must align with the purposes of Jehovah-Jireh so that through our sowing we open a channel of righteousness, praise to the Lord, and a flow from God's kingdom. As the Lord transforms our hearts, our compassion undoubtedly will grow. However, we are not called to chase every need; rather, the Lord invites us to partner with him as we seek his vision.

Let's consider practical ways to live lifestyles of generosity. We have discussed the foundational principles: understanding firstfruits and the principle of flow, pursuing the grace of giving, and sowing generously. Yet we still can be challenged when we see a specific, legitimate need where we can help. Is the Lord specifically directing us to this need, or possibly even away from it? How much should we give? We also see opportunities where ministries have the potential to advance God's kingdom and impact people's lives. Legitimate kingdom-building ministries are everywhere, and they always seem to need more money. We should seek the wisdom of the Lord, specifically for our part in giving to these ministries, so that our efforts will be aligned with his vision.

Our relationship with God will never be formulaic, nor will determining his direction for us as we join him in blessing others through generosity. There may be times when we choose to bless someone or some situation with a gift born from our compassion. That's great. There also may be times when we feel we have genuinely heard from the Lord. Then proceed as directed! However, often we find ourselves seeking his direction as we weigh good stewardship, a lifestyle of generosity, and the vision the Lord would have for us. For those situations, here are some practical approaches that will help us stay aligned with the principles and also seek the mind of Christ and the heart of the Spirit to direct us in expressions of generosity.

We know that even with all we have discussed, our tendency can be to add a layer of stress or anxiety about when to give and the amount we should give. We ask ourselves, "Is this amount too little, so that I am not doing what God desires and what is needed?" Or we ask, "Is it too big, so that I will not be able to meet my other obligations and commitments or be a good steward of what I have?" God does not intend to add this dimension of stress to our giving. Recall that right after encouraging us to sow generously so that we may reap generously, Scripture states, *"Each man should give what he has decided in his heart to give, not reluctantly or under compulsion, for God loves a cheerful giver"* (2 Corinthians 9:6-7). God's desire is for us to give generously, even extravagantly, while having peace and excitement about it at the same time. Any expressions of love for God and for others whom he also loves should bring us great joy.

Seeking The Lord's Direction for Giving

Using the framework created by the principles we have covered thus far, here are some guidelines to help align ourselves with God's vision for giving. They provide some structure for sorting out the principles, the needs, and our thoughts and circumstances. This guide can help us reach the point where we feel confident in the Lord's direction and our response. Then we can fully enter into the joy of giving cheerfully.

1. Don't compare. One of our first reactions when we think about what to give is to compare ourselves with others. When people share a story of how God provided for them or led them in some dramatic way, our gut reaction can be, "What about me?" God has not given everyone the ability to give the same amount because we simply don't have the same situations. He also calls us and gifts us all differently. Yet God always wants us to open a heavenly flow of resources through a spirit of generosity. Therefore his interest is always our hearts. Rejoice with those God blesses and even those he richly blesses. Be thankful they are part of his family too and generously sharing with others. Ask the Lord to show you what your part is and avoid the anxiety of comparing yourself or your gifts to others. It is true the stories of others can inspire us, and the Lord can use them to challenge us. But we need to respond out of encouragement, conviction, and challenged faith, not out of guilt or trying to measure up.

2. Invest. When we think of giving a gift, it's natural to think of what we will be giving up. However, this keeps our eyes on ourselves. Instead, we must turn our focus outward and consider what we are investing in. Think of the people's lives that will be touched and impacted through your gift, just as your life has been touched by others in the past. Consider your gifts of generosity investments in others, the family of God, and the kingdom of God for the benefit of others.

3. Revelation, not Reason. We can give based on reason, our normal starting point. We consider what we have, figure out what is "reasonable," and give that amount. It takes no faith to give by reason. Reason simply asks, "What can I afford?" However, instead of reason, we should give based on revelation. We seek the Lord for his vision, rather than give simply on the basis of the needs we see. We ask, "Lord, what and where do you want to give through me?" This requires faith. When we make giving a matter of prayer and faith, our decision becomes an act of worship. Revelation giving requires that we put our trust in God. It requires that we know him as Jehovah-Jireh, the God Abraham experienced when he chose to worship and obey. Abraham is known as the father of our faith. The Lord revealed himself to Abraham in that dramatic encounter in Genesis 22, but we have the added benefit of seeing the revealed glory of Abraham's journey and God's entire redemptive plan down through the ages and through all the godly people of faith. Moreover, we live on this side of the cross, which means we have the Scriptures, the mind of Christ, and the presence of the Holy Spirit to guide and direct us.

Here are four questions and corresponding Scriptures that can help lead and guide us as we seek God's vision and revelation.

A. Will I give based on reason or revelation? Is my gift just what I think I can afford or is it what God wants to give through me?

They gave as much as they were able, and even beyond their ability. (2 Corinthians 8:3)

I will not sacrifice to the Lord my God ... [an] offering that costs me nothing. (2 Samuel 24:24)

B. Does the amount I'm considering really stretch my faith?

But just as you excel in everything – in faith, in speech, in knowledge, in complete earnestness and in your love ... see that you also excel in this grace of giving. (2 Corinthians 8:7)

C. Will this amount demonstrate how much I love God and my desire to see others blessed?

This service that you perform is not only supplying the needs of God's people but is also overflowing in many expressions of thanks to God. (2 Corinthians 9:12)

D. Have I sincerely prayed, asking God to direct me in this decision? Do I trust God's faithfulness?

And God is able to make all grace abound to you, so that in all things at all times, having all that you need, you will abound in every good work. (2 Corinthians 9:8)

4. Give yourself time. Don't rush your decision. Sometimes there are emergency situations in which we may feel compelled to help. May God bless everyone who responds in those situations. More often, however, spending time with the Lord will bring clarity, direction, confirmation, and peace. As we earnestly pray about a concern or need that is on our heart, we give God room to confirm his vision. Sometimes his vision will be even bigger than we initially thought. At other times we may have a growing unsettledness that should cause us to question our initial thoughts. The Lord may not always speak specific numbers or details to us, but he has a wonderful way of moving upon our spirit. We can feel confirmation and conviction of a thought or decision we have made, and this allows us to proceed confidently. But at times we can feel unsettled, and we should not ignore this. We can feel stirred, inspired, and motivated, and we can feel great peace resting upon us about a decision to give generously, even when it may not make sense in the natural world. In fact, a great confirmation can be when we experience that level of peace, even though the situation may not be comfortable.

5. Decide, and rely on God. If we choose to live a lifestyle of generosity, and if we follow the Lord's direction and vision and do not chase need, then our gift of sowing generously can be given with a cheerful heart. We are confident in the Lord and his flow. We confidently know he will provide seed for the sower and even increase our store of seed. A lifestyle of generosity definitely will end up stretching our faith, and that's great! That's part of the increased harvest of righteousness awaiting us.

Money Seeds

We sow seed, and seed is for growing the harvest. Seed is not the harvest itself. The seed we sow is not the fullness of the gift of blessing that has been given. When we give to bless others, we help to meet an initial need;

but if the spirit of generosity is flowing, our gift is also seed that will produce a much greater harvest to come.

A number of years ago my wife, Pam, began a practice that I have since adopted as well. We each carry a specific amount of money that we call a *money seed*. This money is tucked away in our wallets. We do not use this money for ourselves. When we become aware of a particular situation as we are talking to or ministering to someone, we always have a money seed available to plant into that situation or that life. It is not a large amount of money, although it can be helpful in the moment. The significance is that this money is a seed. When we give (or sow) this seed, we pray over it and the recipient. We pray that the seed will bring forth a breakthrough and even a great harvest. We believe the seed that is sown is good and in the right soil will produce a bounty. We also know that presented with the right heart, it will encourage the recipient and build faith for the harvest to come.

We desire to release heaven's flow with this blessing and also to bring hope and expectation of God's faithful provision into the situation. Whether our gifts are relatively small seeds or financially substantial, understanding the Scriptures that speak of sowing and reaping and believing in a harvest of righteousness can transform a sense of hopelessness into confidence in Jehovah-Jireh and bring peace in the midst of trying circumstances. When we truly believe in God's kingdom and his economy, we can choose to live and give with a different perspective from the world around us. We have the privilege and responsibility of allowing God's heavenly resources to flow through us as we live lifestyles of generosity with the grace of giving.

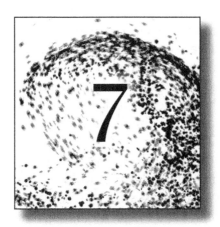

I Got This

So Abraham called that place The Lord Will Provide. And to this day it is said, "On the mountain of the Lord it will be provided." (Genesis 22:14)

My wife, Pam, has observed that when she genuinely asks questions of the Lord, he rarely answers the question, but he always settles the matter. I've experienced that truth on a number of occasions, and it accurately describes the following situation.

"I got this" is what I distinctly heard.

I was facing a situation for which I could see no solution. I knew we could not continue the course we were on. I also knew (or so it seemed) that there was no way to change the course. I desperately needed an unforeseeable resolution, and I had been desperate for quite some time.

I gathered a small group of men to intercede with me, and I shared with them the need for breakthrough in this matter, which now was beginning to overwhelm me. All of a sudden as we were praying, I heard "I got this." I opened my eyes. The rest of the men continued praying, unaware of my encounter. I chuckled to myself because it seemed that if this was the Lord, he would have worded it better. He would have said, "I have this," or "Thus sayeth the Lord, I have this," but not the colloquial "I got this." Yet I knew it was the Lord, and he was answering my cry. He may not have given the answer to the problem or a clear solution, but he was letting me know he would bring the resolution. I could count on him to settle the matter. In fact, by faith (*"being sure of what we hope for and certain of what we do not see"* [Hebrews 11:1]) the matter was already settled.

Understanding *Jehovah-Jireh*

Jehovah-Jireh is one of the names of the Lord we find in the Old Testament. It's translated into English as "The Lord Will Provide." We often use this Hebrew name when referring to the Lord as our provider, but we narrow our perspective if we think it refers only to the Lord's provision for finances and, even more specifically, quantity. Although accurate, this is an extremely limited and narrow understanding. If Jehovah-Jireh speaks only to the relationship with our Lord as he helps us with money, then we fail to grasp not only a great name for our God but also the profound truth conveyed by that name.

We are introduced to *Jehovah-Jireh* in the story we discussed in chapter 2, when the Lord asked Abraham to offer his son Isaac as a burnt offering. Previously we considered the perspective that Isaac was a firstfruit of the promised Israelite nation, Jesus the Messiah, and ultimately all the believing children of God. Now let's look at the story again, this time examining the depth and context of the story to see what led Abraham to create this new name for God. Jehovah-Jireh must refer to much more than provision and speak to much more than finances, because we are actually introduced to this name for our Lord in a story about worship and obedience.

Worship

In fact, the first occurrence in the Bible of the word *worship* is found in this story, when Abraham told his servants he and his son Isaac were going to the mountaintop to worship. The book of Genesis has twenty-one chapters preceding this story, all depicting early mankind and his relationship with God. Those early chapters contain the grand stories of Adam and Eve, Abel, Noah, and even much of Abraham's life. Yet, the actual word *worship* first occurs here. In some of the previous stories, worship is present and even quite central. My perspective is that here the Lord is saying, "Now, let me teach you about worship." The Lord instructs Abraham to sacrifice Isaac, and Abraham calls it an act of worship.

Some time later God tested Abraham. He said to him, "Abraham!"

"Here I am," he replied.

Then God said, "Take your son, your only son, Isaac, whom you love, and go to the region of Moriah. Sacrifice him there as a burnt offering

on one of the mountains I will tell you about."
(Genesis 22:1-2)

The very first thing we see here is that God was actually testing Abraham. Scripture makes that point clear to us, although I doubt Abraham understood it that way, at least not at the moment. God also made it clear that he knew exactly what he was asking Abraham. He was telling Abraham, "Take your son … yes, I know he is your one and only son … yes, I know he is the one you deeply love … yes, I know he is Isaac, the promised son you and I named because of the absolutely laughable circumstances of his miracle birth. Yes, take *that* son and sacrifice him to me as a burnt offering."

What must Abraham have thought? If he and his wife Sarah laughed at the ridiculous notion of bearing a son in their very old age, then how much more was this request beyond comprehension. The Lord's promise to Abraham was not that he would have one son but rather that his descendants would outnumber the stars of the sky. Sacrificing Isaac would not only destroy a life and a miracle, but it would also eliminate the only hope for the Lord's promise to ever be fulfilled. How could the Lord bring forth millions of descendants when the root of the family tree was destroyed before it even had a chance to grow? How could God ask Abraham to destroy the very gift he so miraculously gave to him? How could God ask Abraham to sacrifice the one who was so precious to him, the one he loved so dearly?

The Lord already had made it perfectly clear to Abraham that it would be through Isaac only that the promise would be fulfilled. Abraham had tried to bring forth offspring (and the Lord's promise) through his wife's servant girl Hagar, and the result was the birth of Ishmael. Abraham asked the Lord to bless

Ishmael, for he felt he could no longer hold out hope for Isaac's miracle birth (Genesis 17). The Lord told Abraham he would bless Ishmael, but the promise would be fulfilled through the yet unborn Isaac. Thus there seemed to be nothing rational, logical, or even consistent between Abraham's decades-long journey that ultimately led to Isaac's birth and this latest command of the Lord to sacrifice the promised son. So how did Abraham respond?

Obey

> *Early the next morning Abraham got up and saddled his donkey. He took with him two of his servants and his son Isaac. When he had got enough wood for the burnt offering, he set out for the place God had told him about. On the third day Abraham looked up and saw the place in the distance. He said to his servants, "Stay here with the donkeys while I and the boy go over there. We will worship and then we will come back to you."* (Genesis 22:3-5).

Abraham responded the same way he had always responded on his journey of faith. It's the only way he knew how. Abraham obeyed. When God first asked Abraham to pack up his family and move to a distant land, Abraham obeyed immediately (Genesis 12). Then, after twenty-four years of waiting for the promised son, the Lord instructed Abraham to be circumcised. The burden of waiting had become nearly unbearable to Abraham, while the unfulfilled promise moved beyond an act of faith to the ridiculous. I'm sure he didn't want to be circumcised at ninety-nine years of age, yet the Scripture says he got up *"that very day"* and obeyed the Lord (Genesis 17). Now facing another unwelcomed and unexplainable instruction from the Lord, Abraham remained unwavering in his commitment to the Lord. He immediately obeyed. There appeared to be no hesitation, as verse 3 begins, *"Early the next morning."* In the face of unanswerable questions and gut-wrenching emotions, Abraham set out to obey the Lord.

For over two days Abraham walked, his son by his side, in full obedience and most undoubtedly in deep agony. On the third day, off in the distance he identified the place for the sacrifice. He told his servants he and Isaac were going to *worship*. This is the dramatic entrance of the word *worship* into the Holy Bible.

Think of how casually most of us use the word *worship*. In our Christian culture, we often reduce it to mean praise music. We critique it by how it makes us feel or to what degree we are able to enter into the expressions of the songs. We hear or even say things such as, "What a great time of worship. I really enjoy those songs. I'm really able to enter in."

Corporate praise is a wonderful expression of worship, but biblical worship as it is introduced through this story is substantially different. I doubt Abraham expected to complete this act of worship feeling spiritually and emotionally warm inside. His expectations and goals for this worship experience were not self-centered but rather God-centered through obedience and faith. Abraham's worship was an act of obedience, a commitment of faith, and a deep sacrifice.

The Lord Himself Will See to It

How did worship lead Abraham to an understanding of the Lord as his provider? The story continues.

Abraham took the wood for the burnt offering and placed it on his son Isaac, and he himself carried the fire and the knife. As the two of them went on together, Isaac spoke up and said to his father Abraham, "Father?" "Yes, my son?" Abraham replied. "The fire and wood are here," Isaac said, "but where is the lamb for the burnt offering?" Abraham answered, "God himself will provide the lamb for the burnt offering, my son." And the two of them went on together. (Genesis 22:6-8)

Isaac obviously had seen burnt offerings before, so the question was understandable: where is the lamb? The real question was, what will be the sacrifice? Abraham's response to his son's question was accurate and straightforward. We can try to make it superspiritual, or we can view it as a quick-witted dismissal of the obvious reality facing the father-son team. However, I see it simply as Abraham's honest response born from his lifelong faith journey. *God himself would provide.*

Throughout Abraham's life, he had chosen to trust the Lord's direction, regardless of how challenging or outrageous it seemed or how contrary it appeared to his surrounding circumstances. Now he chose to obey with that same faith. He trusted that the God he had chosen to listen to, be faithful to, and follow would once again come through. I seriously doubt he had any expectation of finding a ram caught in a thicket on top of the mountain. We don't know what he was thinking. The author of Hebrews said Abraham reasoned that, if necessary, the Lord could even raise Isaac from the dead (Hebrews 11:19). Abraham did tell the servants with him that he and Isaac were going to worship, and he said, "**We** *will come back to you.*" We also see later in the story that Abraham was fully prepared to obey this instruction of the Lord to its fateful end.

We don't fully know how he thought this unprecedented action was going to play out. Personally, I doubt Abraham had an answer. I see a man obeying a God he deemed worthy of his worship. That included following his Lord into the unknown because Abraham's confidence was not in knowing the outcome but rather in the Lord's covenant relationship. And that had never failed because the Lord had always remained faithful. So Abraham's response to Isaac was his straightforward and honest explanation of what would transpire, *"God himself will provide."*

The Hebrew word translated *"provide"* means *to see to it.* The Hebrew reads, *"The Lord himself will see to it."* Abraham was telling Isaac that the God of the promise, the God of the covenant, would himself see to it. He would see to the sacrifice, and he would see to the promise. The translation *"will provide"* can leave us thinking more literally about the sacrificial lamb, especially when we know the rest of the story. Although Isaac's question focused on the animal to be sacrificed, Abraham responded instead from his lifelong covenant and his consistent experience that directed and sustained his life: "Isaac my son, *the Lord himself will see to it."*

What does our relationship with the Lord look like? We can state what we believe. We can describe our personal commitment to study, prayer, worship, or service. We can declare our deep love for the Lord. However, when difficult situations or circumstances strip away the layers and leave our relationship bare and exposed; when hard questions and disappointments crush our faith leaving only the core; when expectations and God-inspired hope go unfulfilled or even crash and burn right in front of us; what are we left with?

Hebrews 12 states that everything that can be shaken will be shaken so that only the unshakable will remain. Do we have an unshakable core relationship with our Lord? Will it stand up to shaking? Will we be so secure in our relationship that even during the shaking we will still choose to worship?

"Since we are receiving a kingdom that cannot be shaken, let us be thankful, and so worship God acceptably with reverence and awe" (Hebrews 12:28). Two of the very first building blocks of this unshakable kingdom were Abraham's faith and his son Isaac, the firstfruit of the promise. In this story, the formative foundation of God's kingdom on earth was being shaken to the core, but Abraham's covenant relationship with God remained unshakable. It was the only thing left (if Isaac had been sacrificed), but it was unshakable. Abraham said, *"I* will worship, and *God* will see to it." This was Abraham's only option if he was going to believe that God would keep his covenant to be his God, and if Abraham was going to choose to be his people.

Abraham's Test

Abraham continued on to the place for the sacrifice. He was resolved to maintain his covenant commitment with his faithful Lord. He built an altar and arranged the wood. Then Abraham bound his son, laid him on the altar, and raised the knife.

> *But the angel of the Lord called out to him from heaven. "Abraham! Abraham!"*
>
> *"Here I am," he replied.*

> *"Do not lay a hand on the boy," he said. "Do not do anything to him. Now I know that you fear God, because you have not withheld from me your son, your only son." Abraham looked up and there in a thicket he saw a ram caught by its horns. He went over and took the ram and sacrificed it as a burnt offering instead of his son. So Abraham called that place The Lord Will Provide. And to this day it is said, "On the mountain of the Lord it will be provided."* (Genesis 22:11-14)

Abraham's journey of faith, trust, and obedience passed the test. He remained faithful to the covenant the Lord had made with him. He trusted the Lord to be faithful, and his obedience allowed the sacrifice to be an acceptable offering to the Lord. Here we are introduced to this name of God as Abraham called this mountaintop location *Jehovah-Jireh,* "The Lord Will Provide." Remember that the broader understanding of the word *Jireh* is *"to see to it."* Specifically, it means the Lord himself will see to it. Abraham put his whole confidence in the Lord's ability to see to it. The Lord promised to make Abraham the father of nations. God then initiated the fulfillment of the promise through Isaac. When the Lord then called Abraham to sacrifice Isaac, he was testing him to see whether he would put his deepest hope in Isaac, the gift from the Lord, or in the Lord himself, the provider of the gift. Abraham trusted the Lord to provide, to see to it. Abraham passed the test.

Let's reflect on the promise the Lord put before Abraham, which was not simply that he would have a son in his old age. The promise was that Abraham's descendants would outnumber the stars of the sky and through him the whole world would be blessed. This promise included the coming Messiah, Jesus. It includes all those who believe and are grafted into the family of God, descendants of Abraham and Isaac. We discussed how Isaac was the firstfruits, an offering to the Lord of the first of the harvest in worship of him. We recognize and declare that it is the Lord who is our Jehovah-Jireh. The firstfruits must be offered for the remaining fullness of the harvest of nations to come forth.

Now, think about the ram with its horns caught in a thicket. Was a ram an adequate sacrifice for the great harvest of God's children, who would be born and redeemed into his family? The only sacrifice adequate for that great harvest was the actual firstfruit itself, which had to be Isaac. The ram was not an adequate substitute for Isaac. It never could have been. But what was God testing? He was not testing the worthiness of the sacrifice. He was not testing to see if the burnt offering was acceptable. He clearly told Abraham what the acceptable burnt offering would be, and it could only be Isaac. Abraham said to Isaac the Lord himself would see to it there would be an acceptable offering, but that acceptable offering was not the ram. The Lord was testing Abraham's *heart*. Abraham's willingness to worship and obey qualified the offering and made it acceptable before the Lord. The Lord saw to it in Abraham's obedience. He was tested, and he passed the test.

In the next paragraph, the Lord reiterated to Abraham the extent of the promise and declared once again that it would indeed come forth because Abraham had obeyed the Lord (Genesis 22:18). Interestingly, this is also the first occurrence in the Bible of the word *obey*. This story introduces us to both words: *worship* and *obey*. We long to know and experience God as our Jehovah-Jireh, our provider, the Lord who sees to it. We recognize through this story that our part is to worship

God and to obey him. Then we will find him as the Lord who himself will see to it.

"I Got This"

I distinctly heard, "I got this" that night in my office with my prayer brothers. I believe the Lord was saying to me, "I am your Jehovah-Jireh. I am the Lord who himself will see to it. I am Jehovah–I Got This." That's my new understanding, my new translation for Jehovah-Jireh: *Jehovah–I Got This.* This is exactly what happened in my situation. Where there seemed to be no way forward and no way out, the Lord became my Jehovah-I Got This. It required that I continue to journey in faith, trust, and obedience. It required that I continue to worship him as my Lord and provider regardless of the situation and circumstances. And then, where there was no way, he made a way, because he is *Jehovah-I Got This.*

God is a covenant-keeping God. He is true to his word, and he is true to his nature. We may be tested at times, and our faith and trust in his goodness will require obedience and even worship. It is precisely in those times when we need to confidently know our God, "The Lord Will Provide." We need to know "Our Lord will see to it."

Too often we find ourselves testing the nature of God. We try to test the ability of God to provide or at least to provide for us. We think, "I'll test you, God; and if you provide, if you come through, if you see to it, then you will be a God I can put my trust in. Then you will be a God worthy of my worship and obedience." Abraham did not test God. Rather he responded to the test of God with an immediate decision to worship and obey.

Where are our hearts? Do we trust God, or do we feel we need to test him first? Do we believe in a God we can only partially trust, one we can't fully depend on to provide for us? Do we fear that God might ask us to sacrifice more than we want to, more than we should be asked to? We can know our Jehovah-Jireh. He will provide. He will see to it. It is not for us to test a covenant-keeping, trustworthy God. Rather, we put our faith to the test when we align our hearts through worship and obedience so that the Lord can say to us, "I got this."

Test Me in This

"Bring the whole tithe into the storehouse, that there may be food in my house. Test me in this," says the Lord Almighty, "and see if I will not throw open the floodgates of heaven and pour out so much blessing that there will not be room enough to store it." (Malachi 3:10)

"Test me in this," declared the Lord, boldly and in no uncertain terms. But we just concluded the previous chapter by stating, "It is not for us to test a covenant-keeping, trustworthy God." So, which is it?

In the story of Jehovah-Jireh, God expressly tested Abraham to determine whether he would trust God and chose to worship and obey him no matter what the circumstances. Yet in this passage from Malachi, God invited the Israelite nation to test his faithfulness. God himself put the challenge before them, and the subject was specifically the tithe. Let's take a deeper look at this Scripture passage, what the tithe is, what the test is, and what God intends for us through this practice.

"Test me in this ... and see if I will not throw open the floodgates of heaven and pour out so much blessing that there will not be room enough to store it" (Malachi 3:10), the Lord said. Ironically, we usually start with the exact opposite thought. We say to the Lord, "Test me, God. Bless me with finances. Provide me with what I need, and grace me with your blessings, and see if I won't honor you with my whole tithe." It can't be both ways, can it? Does God place his hope in *our* promise to him, or does he ask us to place our hope in *his* promise?

This is a constant challenge for us. We feel we need to *know* so that we can *believe*. We need to understand something before we can put our faith in it. We say, "Once I understand, I will be able to believe." However, the Lord says, "Believe, and you will begin the journey of understanding." Malachi 3 presents us with this same challenge, in this case specifically regarding giving the whole tithe to the Lord. The challenge is squarely upon us. "Test me in this," said the Lord. "Believe and put your belief into action. You may not understand, but test your faith in me, and begin the journey of understanding."

Before getting to this point and directly addressing tithing, I wanted to first lay a foundation of the principles of God's economy. In order to most clearly understand and embrace the practice of tithing, it is important to establish the principles we have covered throughout the book. Indeed, tithing rests on these principles. We discussed honoring the Lord with firstfruits. Then we shifted our perspective from getting and giving to understanding the principle of flow. We differentiated between poverty and a spirit of poverty, and between prosperity and a spirit of generosity. We examined the story that introduces us to Jehovah-Jireh, where God essentially says, "I got this." And we studied the concept of sowing and reaping. With this foundation, we are now better equipped to openly and honestly look at the practice of tithing. While living a lifestyle of generosity presents us with endless opportunities to sow into the needs of others and therefore the kingdom of God (love your neighbor as yourself), tithing to our church or Christ-following community is our expression of firstfruits we give to the Lord (love the Lord your God).

Malachi 3:6-12

Regarding the practice of tithing, the Lord said, "Test me." He challenged the Israelites to watch what would happen when they brought the tithe, the *whole* tithe, to him in obedience. In fact, the challenge was even bolder than the Lord putting his promise on the line before them. The word of the Lord spoken through Malachi charged the people with actually robbing God. The Lord engaged them, saying, *"You ask, 'How do we rob you?'"* (Malachi 3:8). He responded to the question by pointing out that they were failing to bring the whole tithe. He then declared the full extent of the promise. Not only would the Lord receive the tithe offering and remove the curse that had fallen upon the whole nation, but he would throw open the floodgates of heaven and pour out so much blessing there would not be room enough to store it all. Furthermore, he would protect their crops from pests and cause their fields to yield a great harvest. Even other nations would recognize and admire their land and call the Israelites blessed.

This simple, yet bold declaration from the Lord is a wonderful synopsis of the principles we have been discussing. If we do not respond appropriately to the Lord with our finances, it is nothing short of robbing God. However, the invitation was clear and distinct. The Lord said, "Try me; I'm good for it." The result would be overwhelmingly rewarding.

Simple, clear, and rewarding, right? It's as easy as one, two, three. Yet, all too often we experience the struggle. Even when we have chosen to be faithfully obedient with the tithe, we don't always experience simplicity and ease. We don't always feel we are receiving the promised reward, and guilt is often knocking at the door. Interestingly, we can experience guilt on either side of the practice of tithing. We can faithfully tithe out of a sense of guilt that requires us to be obedient, or we may not be tithing and feeling guilty because of it. Guilt occupies the place where freedom should be. The Lord's instruction may be simple, but that's no guarantee it will be easy.

Understanding Tithing

I can recall a conversation with my mother when I was a young boy. The details are fuzzy, but the feelings remain quite vivid. She handed me a $10 allowance, an increased amount I assume was due to my age. I remember responding, "I'm glad you taught me to tithe a dime when I received one dollar, because it's hard to think of giving a whole dollar as a tithe." I've experienced that incremental challenge many times over the years. I remain grateful to my mother, because I know it still helps me make the decision to hold to my commitment. I don't have to decide whether or not to tithe each week or each paycheck. I made the decision to tithe a long time ago.

Our goal has been to gain understanding and perspective that will give us freedom in the area of finances. *"It is for freedom that Christ has set us free"* (Galatians 5:1). Tithing has that same goal. If the subject irritates us, or our experience or attempt to faithfully tithe has been frustrating, then we are not settled, and we certainly are not free. In general, that lack of freedom can come either from bad teaching and poor understanding (that is, the value of giving and tithing has been skewed or completely dismissed) or from our own issues or dismissiveness of the subject. Let's face it; we don't always want to face it. But tithing is precisely where we tangibly engage the wonderful principles we have discussed, along with their freedoms and rewards. If you have embraced the principles of the economy of God's kingdom, I encourage you to remain in that understanding. Do not let the practical application of tithing nudge you to revert back to this world's economy and its limitations.

Throughout the world nearly all commerce is administered through a monetary system. The imagery throughout the Bible of firstfruits, harvest, sowing seeds and reaping righteousness, etc. is wonderful and valuable as we attempt to grasp the principles and understanding of God's economy. The visual stories present practical pictures, whether they are actual historical events or parables. However, most of us do not live in an agrarian society, so our commerce is through money. Even for the few of us who farm or still produce a product from our own hands and labor, we still administer our product or harvest primarily through an exchange of money. Money may not provide for us quite as dramatic imagery as an actual harvest, but it does simplify these principles into a common commodity.

While I won't attempt to do an exhaustive study of tithing, I want to look briefly at the practice of tithing that we find throughout the Bible. First, tithing is straightforward and not an obscure teaching tucked away in a corner of the Bible in confusing language. Second, there really isn't a lot of explanation and teaching about the tithe. The explanation is understood as an expression of firstfruits, which we have already discussed at length. Most of the passages are instructional, teaching the agrarian-based Israelites how to actually bring the tithe. Third, we don't tend to struggle with the understanding of tithing or what it means. Rather, we struggle with trusting God to be faithful; and if we can't trust God, then the foundation for tithing is unstable.

We found our initial encounter with firstfruits (the principle behind tithing) in the story of Cain and Abel in Genesis 4. The first record of a tithe gift appears a few chapters later in Genesis 14, where Abraham gave a tithe to King Melchizedek. Abraham's nephew Lot had been taken captive. When Abraham defeated Lot's captors and rescued him, he also plundered the fallen army. On his return home, he met Melchizedek, the king of Salem. We know nothing about this king except that he's referred to as the *"priest of God Most High"* (Genesis 14:18). He blessed Abraham and praised God for Abraham's victory, at which point Abraham gave the king a tenth of the plunder.

The New Testament book of Hebrews recounts this ancient story as a teaching illustration because Melchizedek resembles the Son of God. *Melchizedek* means "king of righteousness," and *king of Salem* means "king of peace." Even before God gave the laws through Moses and formed the Israelite nation, the tithe gift already had been practiced by the patriarch of that very nation hundreds of years earlier. The Hebrews 7 retelling of this story identifies Abraham's gift as the forerunner of what the law would eventually reflect — that the people would provide a tenth of what they had for the priests. Abraham didn't give the firstfruits of an actual harvest, but he had acquired new provision (the plunder), and he enacted the tithe as his firstfruits offering. Abraham was maintaining a channel for the flow of God's provision.

The word *tithe* simply means tenth. The firstfruits gift both honors God for his provision and declares our trust in God for his continued faithfulness and his full provision to come. The tithe provides us with a practical expression by which to faithfully offer firstfruits to the Lord. Actual instructions for the tithe are found in the laws recorded in Leviticus, Numbers, and Deuteronomy. They can appear to be a complex web of details describing how and where to bring the tithe. At the core, the instruction remains this simple: bring a tenth to the house of the Lord for the priests to administer.

> *"A tithe of everything from the land, whether grain from the soil or fruit from the trees, belongs to the Lord; it is holy to the Lord ... Every tithe of the herd or flock will be holy to the Lord"* *(Leviticus 27:30-32).*

The tithe continues to be referenced throughout the historical books, the wisdom literature, and the books of prophecy, which complete the Old Testament. Tithing was understood and practiced by the Israelite nation.

Tithing Today

Some people question whether the obligation to tithe continues with the new covenant of our salvation through faith in Jesus Christ. Our righteousness is found only through the exchange of our filthy rags of unrighteousness for Christ's pure garments of righteousness through faith in him. As such, we no longer observe many of the requirements of the law to maintain our relationship and right standing with God, such as ceremonial cleansing or many of the sacrificial offerings. Does this include the tithe? To answer this we need to understand the relationship between the law of the Old Testament and the new covenant of grace available to us now through Jesus.

In what has become known as the Sermon on the Mount, Jesus declared, *"Do not think that I have come to abolish the Law or the Prophets; I have not come to abolish them but to fulfill them"* (Matthew 5:17). Jesus then proceeded to give examples of how the new covenant "fulfills" the law. For instance, the law said do not murder (one of the Ten Commandments), but Jesus declared that even if you call your brother a fool you are revealing the sin residing in your heart. Jesus did not abolish the sixth commandment, saying that it no longer applies. The law established a baseline of conduct to govern our relationships with God and each other. The law governs our conduct, while Jesus introduced a new covenant based on internal governance. This is possible only through the victory of Christ and the presence of the Holy Spirit residing within us and transforming us from the inside out. With the new covenant, God does not measure our conduct but our hearts. God and his principles remain the same, but he commands us to love our neighbor as ourselves. The law guarded that value by declaring that we were not to murder one another. That same value is now pursued by our transformed hearts to love our neighbors.

Jesus taught this external-to-internal shift through a number of examples in his Sermon on the Mount. Though not specifically using the tithe or the principle of firstfruits as one of his illustrations, the same understanding of the new covenant and its fulfillment of the law applies. The practice of tithing in the Old Testament ensured the value of honoring God with firstfruits and declaring that our hope and trust remain in him and his provision. As we receive and embrace the new covenant of grace, we do not forgo the tithe. Rather we "fulfill" its underlying value as we are transformed into the likeness of Christ, so that we overflow with love for our Lord and with compassion for others. In the new covenant, the tithe simply remains the baseline for how we handle our resources.

Jesus was asked what the greatest commandment was. He replied that it is to love the Lord your God with all your heart, soul, mind, and strength. Then he added that the second greatest commandment is to love your neighbor as yourself (Mark 12:28-31). Jesus was quoting from the Old Testament and describing a complete devotion to God from all dimensions of our lives. The fact is that much of our lives (our time, effort, and energy) translate to finances. Even if money is not our focus, priority, or even purpose, it's still the commodity we use. Loving the Lord our God with complete devotion includes loving him with what we acquire, earn, and produce. The tithe (our firstfruits offering) declares our gratitude to God and our confident dependence on God for all we have and all we will need.

Jesus also echoed the Old Testament in calling us to love our neighbors as ourselves. We express this through a lifestyle of generosity. It's helpful to recognize the difference between our tithe devotion to God and our God-inspired desire to help and bless others. Jesus stated that the combination of the two (love God, love your neighbor) is the foundation for all other instruction, but they are two different things. So also is the tithe distinctly different from generosity. The tithe is an undesignated gift and declaration to the Lord that recognizes his lordship and his faithful provision as our heavenly Father. We do not give it with strings attached or with demands for how it should be used. Tithing is an offering to the Lord that represents our gratitude and devotion to him. For nearly all of us, our tithe is as an offering to the specific church or fellowship that provides our body-of-Christ community.

The Posture of Tithing

The tithe is a percentage, since it is a tenth of what we earn, acquire, or produce. However, the principle behind tithing is a posture, not a percentage. When Cain brought his gift to the Lord, it may have been an acceptable amount or percentage. However, the story indicates Cain's heart attitude was unacceptable to the Lord. He brought some of his crop, while Abel brought the first and the best. The percentage is not mentioned; the posture, or heart attitude, is highlighted. Tithing presents us with a framework within which we maintain a posture of honoring God with our first and best. Our hearts must desire to love the Lord our God. We use a percentage as a baseline, but we posture our hearts in an act of worship.

Let's also address here some language and perspectives commonly used to describe the tithe that are not helpful or even accurate. Have you heard it said that all we have is the Lord's and he only asks for 10 percent and lets us keep 90 percent? That sounds like a good deal, and it's often presented as a way to encourage us to give while still allowing us to feel good about our situation or the commandment to tithe. However, such an approach to tithing is the wrong focus. Feeling good about what we get to keep is not the goal of tithing. Worshiping God is our goal, because he is faithful and will provide all that we need at all times for all things. I also don't think it's accurate to consider that everything we have is actually the Lord's. As believers, we become citizens of God's kingdom, and we bring all we have into the kingdom. Also, everything we have ultimately comes from the Lord's faithfulness to us. He either provides for us or gives us the ability to provide (Deuteronomy 8). In that sense, all we have belongs to God's kingdom. However, what we have is ours and our responsibility—ours to keep or ours to give. We worship and honor the Lord by tithing from what we have, not by simply giving back to God what already belongs to him.

There may be occasions when we actually do have the opportunity and responsibility to steward the Lord's resources. Yet, as we acquire, earn, and produce resources for ourselves, God delights in our being good stewards of our resources (through gratitude and generosity) with the same spirit and heart attitude he has. He desires for us to employ kingdom principles that will allow his economy to flow through us.

When I gave my boys allowances while they were growing up, it would have been controlling for me to determine how they would use the money. My desire was to instill in them principles for being good stewards of what they had. My desire was not to manage their money and dictate their actions. As a father, my delight was to instill in them principles that would allow them to flourish in their own experience and expressions of good stewardship. We are not obligated to tithe to a controlling heavenly Father. Tithing is not simply a formula to appease God. We posture our hearts in gratitude and trust before the Lord, and we express that posture through the practical, tangible action of giving the tithe, which aligns us with our Jehovah-Jireh.

The Value of Tithing

The value of tithing far exceeds the financial contribution and the percentage. It is the practical, tangible action of the principles we have been addressing throughout this book. With the tithe we honor God with our firstfruits offering, which opens the flow for the full harvest. The tithe also aligns our hearts with God's heart. He declares that he will bless those who are faithful. In fact, the Lord's encouragement to those who are faithful with little is that they will have the privilege to be faithful with much, and that encompasses far more than money.

In the parable where Jesus revealed this truth, the workers who were faithful with a little money were then granted governance over whole cities (Luke 19). The apostle Paul even stated that the tithe (from rightly positioned hearts) will bring a blessing upon all the rest of what we have: *"If the part of the dough offered as firstfruits is holy, then the whole batch is holy"* (Romans 11:16). Understanding the tithe as a percentage may produce a practical, tangible action, but it is the posture of tithing that allows it to open a flow of the economy of the Lord's kingdom.

The bold simplicity of Malachi 3 is a wonderful synopsis of the principles we have been discussing. "Test me in this," says the Lord. A trusted pastor friend recently suggested that we never really keep the tithe for ourselves. Either we offer it to the Lord, or the enemy steals it. Here in Malachi the Lord presented this truth. When we bring the full tithe, pests will not devour our crops, and our fields will yield a good harvest. We make a mistake when we think we cannot afford to give the full tithe offering. We calculate our situation and finances and determine there simply is not 10 percent left over. If we think we are giving the tithe from what is left over, then we may be correct in our calculation. However, that is not the tithe. That is not a firstfruits offering. That is not a posture of tithing. It may very well be that a full 10 percent is not available at the end of our paycheck, yet it is always available at the beginning.

A friend of mine is the chief financial officer for a corporation. He's a certified public accountant who holds an Ivy League MBA. Prior to his current job, he found himself struggling to make ends meet. As his family grew, so did the expenses; and he slowly but increasingly reduced what for years had been a faithful practice of tithing. Conviction set in, so he attacked his budget; but even with his expertise, he couldn't find a way to fully tithe and cover expenses.

Then, a crazy idea came to him. He could discontinue his monthly contribution to his retirement savings plan so that he might fully tithe. As a finance professional, he struggled with the thought. He knew the irresponsibility of not saving and the consequences of losing company-matching contributions. However, the more he wrestled with the idea and prayed about it, the more determined he felt about "testing God." As he describes it, he "was going all in for God," making sure he was bringing the full tithe. "I fully understood that anyone looking at this from a professional viewpoint would ridicule me for being irresponsible. But I stood firm and trusted the Lord," he said. After a few months of faith-filled tithing, my friend was unexpectedly pursued for the position he now holds. God confirmed for this finance "expert" that the tithe does not come from excess resources but from a heart that trusts God.

When our financial situation gets difficult, we may naturally think we have no choice but to forgo our tithe offering. However, that perspective leaves us having to make our ends meet on our own. Let's train our minds (and hearts) to think just the opposite. When our financial situations get difficult, we need God's fatherly care and provision all the more. When we withhold the tithe, we are saying to God, "I can't trust you and your covenant with me, so I'm going to have to do this on my own." When we tithe, we not only recognize and honor our Lord, but we also place our hope in him, opening a channel for his love and care to us.

Do we honor the Lord with the tithe, or do we allow the enemy to steal it? Malachi 3 is the voice of the Lord on this matter. First, if we do not respond appropriately to the Lord with our finances, it is nothing short of robbing God. Second, the invitation is clear and distinct. He says, "Try me; I'm good for it." Third, the result will be overwhelmingly rewarding.

The Freedom of Tithing

God does not invite us to test a formula. We are testing the principles of God's economy and the faithfulness of his heart toward us. If we genuinely believe him, then we surely don't want to rob from him. God invites us to test his faithfulness as our provider. In fact, we should expect that he will provide for us even more completely than we can provide for ourselves. Jesus offered this same perspective when he invited us to seek first the kingdom of God and his righteousness. If we do that, he promised to provide for all of our needs (Matthew 6:33).

God desires our hearts because he desires a covenant relationship with us. We cannot come to him, testing a formula and expecting specific results or rewards. That would be a contract in which we commit to give 10 percent and he commits to taking care of us. Rather than a contract, God invites us into a covenant relationship. Unlike a contractual commitment of what each party will give, in a covenant we give our whole selves. God says, "I'll be your God," and we say, "We'll be your people." When we demonstrate this commitment through the act and posture of tithing, we enter his promise to faithfully provide for us. Furthermore, we don't want to limit the Lord's faithfulness by predetermining what the blessings will look like. His provision is so much more than money. He promises to love us, which includes providing all that we need.

As we take up God's invitation to test him, we also must make room for him to test the sincerity of our hearts in the process, as he asks us, "Do you really and fully trust me? Are you really giving to honor my lordship and protection over your life? Do you really believe I love you and will be able to provide for you as your heavenly Father and your Jehovah-Jireh?" Some of these tests may be necessary to open channels of flow from heaven to us. The Lord may need to remove stumbling blocks in our lives or in our hearts that are clogging the channel and disrupting the flow. Removing blockages allows not only provision to flow but also other blessings of heaven and even the favor of the Lord. Do we believe that with a posture of tithing (not simply a percentage) we can move from stress, nervousness, anxiety, and struggle with finances to a place of favor with the Lord, full of peace, joy, and blessing? Peter wrote, *"Cast all your anxiety on him because he cares for you"* (1 Peter 5:7). By tithing let's cast our cares on him because he cares for us.

> *"But seek first his kingdom and his righteousness, and all these things will be given to you as well."* (Matthew 6:33)

> *"Bring the whole tithe into the storehouse, that there may be food in my house. Test me in this,"* says the Lord Almighty, *"and see if I will not throw open the floodgates of heaven and pour out so much blessing that there will not be room enough to store it."* (Malachi 3:10)

I pray that all who read this will test the Lord's faithfulness, test their own hearts in the process, and walk into the overflowing care, provision, peace, and blessing of the Father God who dearly loves them.

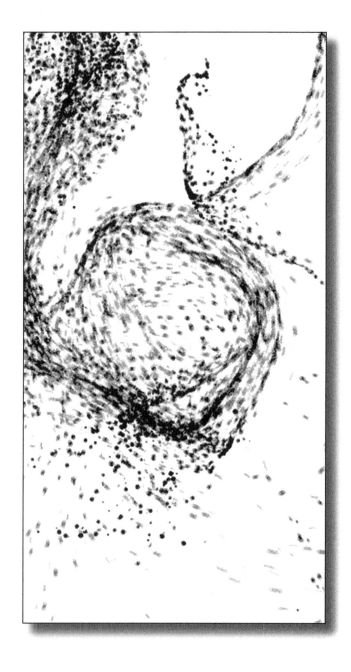

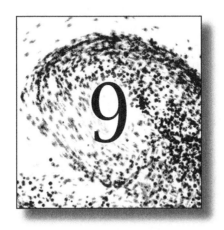

Avoiding the Snares

"Then you will know the truth, and the truth will set you free." (John 8:32)

N ow let's specifically apply kingdom economics to *your* finances in light of *your* faith.

Ugh! Does the thought of such an exercise still deflate you or maybe frighten you? Even if we understand and embrace everything we've addressed, when we turn to our own circumstances, it's easy to conclude that we still must be doing something wrong. In some way we've messed up or we haven't figured it out. Connecting our faith with our finances can cause us to regress back to ninth-grade Algebra class. The teacher's formula on the board always works, but we just can't get X + Y to equal Z. Only this time the

153

teacher is God, the textbook is the Bible, the board is our finances, and the result is an F for failure ... accompanied by disappointment, dissatisfaction, and frustration. We look around the room even more dejected, as we witness the formula working for others but clearly not for us. It hasn't worked in the past, it's not working now, and we're quite certain it won't work in the future either. Guilt presses upon our spirit. Worse than that, we feel defeated. We feel it is inevitable that we are destined to journey through all of life with a failed formula. Lack, less than, and limited is our lot in life. Ugh!

Why do we still struggle? We've laid out God's kingdom economy leading to freedom and flow, yet fear and dejection may still remain and even dominate our thoughts and emotions. Some of our struggles are actually rooted in common misunderstandings and misrepresentations of biblical truths, leaving us ensnared to false teachings and their strongholds. It is imperative that we correct our understanding and dismantle any such strongholds. When we attempt to rationalize our own finances in light of these false teachings, we draw erroneous conclusions that can undermine the whole foundational truth we've sought to establish. Regarding false teachings related to finances, here are examples of what I see as the big three.

1. *"[Jesus said], I have come that they may have life, and have it to the full"* (John 10:10). Therefore, we should expect to be financially comfortable. We should be able to afford all we need (oh, and a little bit more for what we really want).

2. *"The love of money is a root of all kinds of evil"* (1 Timothy 6:10). Therefore, money leads to inevitable corruption, greed, and selfishness.

Poverty is next to godliness. We must not have; and what we do have, we must give away.

3. *"The Scripture says, 'Do not muzzle the ox while it is treading out the grain,' and 'The worker deserves his wages'"* (1 Timothy 5:18). Therefore, we have an obligation to give to the church. We have an obligation to keep the church doors open; and if they close, we are to blame.

The Big Three Errors

Have you heard these teachings or some version of them? Have you been instructed according to these principles, as your mind demands that you measure them against your current financial situation? They are errors, traps, and snares. We can't allow these errant principles to undermine the foundation we've been laying. Let's get things right!

TheScriptures,ofcourse,aretrue,buttheconclusions drawn from the Scriptures above are incomplete, distorted, and in many ways just plain false. The three examples represent the big three errors: God promises financial prosperity, money is evil, and Christian duty requires us to give. These false banners wave over Christians because of erroneous understandings of God's provision and his kingdom's ways. Worse, all three have been used at times to manipulate responses from believers. They come packaged in all manner of teachings, but at the core they ask us to accept inadequate and incomplete perspectives on biblical truths, and they misrepresent God's love, life, and provision for his children and his creation.

The so-called "prosperity gospel" is based on the premise that as we get right with God (most often this means by substantial giving to God, or the presenting church or ministry), we will be rewarded with prosperity. God does desire for all of us to prosper, but a shallow, narrow, and self-serving perspective of how our heavenly Father wants to bless us will only twist, distort, and even invert the purpose and significance of the blessing itself.

Likewise, the opposing perspective that money is evil is antithetical to a believer's genuine sacrificial life and also distorts the Scriptures and the truth. It snuffs out the very heart of the relationship with a loving Father who delights in blessing his children. Possessions are not evil; rather, God judges our heart attitudes concerning what we possess. Jesus' self-sacrificing life reflected in all of us is based in love for others, not in a devaluing of oneself and one's possessions.

The third controlling and errant banner is duty, which allows manipulation, guilt, and shame to be used to club us into obedience. This banner declares that God's law mandates our obedience. Often, layered on top of the law is also an obligation to support the local church. We are told the church must survive, and we have a duty to make it happen. When we reduce the goal of the church to survival, what measure of kingdom advance can we really expect to see?

It is often difficult and challenging to identify the distortion of God's truths while they're being presented or taught. It can be confusing when Scripture is presented as the foundation for the teaching. And when we add to that our own questions, struggles, or confusion, we risk impaired critical thinking and blurred perspective. So let's look closer at the specific examples I've highlighted, each one representing one of the three main snares of false teaching and understanding.

The Error of the Prosperity Gospel

"[Jesus said], I have come that they may have life, and have it to the full" (John 10:10). We are taught that we should expect to be financially comfortable. We should be able to afford all we need (oh, and a little bit more for what we really want).

The King James translation of this verse says we are to *"have [life] more abundantly."* Financial comfort seems an appropriate and accurate understanding of an abundant life. Aren't we supposed to believe this by faith? Jesus didn't come so that we would have minimal life or even adequate life but abundant life. What is abundant life if not a life where we can afford material things, enjoy many experiences and pleasures, participate in many activities, and fulfill all our needs with much left over? Doesn't this define abundant life? Let's look more closely.

We find John 10:10 in the middle of a lengthy illustration describing believers as sheep and Jesus as their good shepherd. The primary purpose of this illustration is to help us understand the relationship between ourselves and our Lord and Savior Jesus. He is our Good Shepherd. He, rather than the sheep, is the focus of the illustration. In the process Jesus spoke of abundant life, which is rooted completely in his being our Good Shepherd. Jesus contrasted himself to all others his sheep might encounter. Whether those others are robbers or even hired hands, there is no comparison to the sheep's relationship with their Good Shepherd. Simply the sound of his voice is enough for them. They will flee the robbers but run to the Good Shepherd.

In this wonderful illustration, abundant life is not a synonym for financial comfort. Rather, it describes the wholeness found in the relationship between the perfect, watchful, caretaking of the perfect Shepherd and his sheep. Our reality is that we are all sheep in need of a good shepherd (Matthew 9:36). No one knows this more than Jesus. That's why he declared, "You can trust me. Unlike the thief who comes to steal, kill, and destroy, I come to bring you life, and the life I bring is abundant."

We have discussed much about God's provision, even in the specifics of our lives and finances. We cannot reduce this wonderful illustration found in John to simply a promise of financial comfort. The invitation is for all of us to respond to the voice of our Good Shepherd. He knows us. He brings us into his sheepfold, and he brings himself (and all that encompasses) to us. He declares that in the intimate relationship with him there will be an abundantly full life.

It may be challenging at times for us to see ourselves as blessed with abundant life. Yet, it is worthwhile to examine our own evaluations, since we tend to use worldly measurements because that is what we know and with which we are most familiar. We also must remember that God works all things together for the good of those who love him (Romans 8:28). We cannot evaluate the promises of God in a moment in time and disregard vital tenets of our Christian worldview such as the fallen world, sin, free will (our own and others), and the "already but not yet" of the full victory in Christ. There may be times when the formula of God's faithful provision may not seem to be working. In those times we turn to the foundational truth of this illustration. We remind ourselves that we have a Good Shepherd. We tune our ear to hear his voice. We rest our life in our relationship with him and remind ourselves that it is an abundant life.

Think of how we would define what we want from an abundant life. Does that look different from the life

Jesus lived while on this earth? Starkly different? He is our Shepherd. He is our Lord and King. He is the Lord of Lords and King of Kings. He is our Savior and the Savior of the world. That sounds like an exceedingly abundant life. Yet he lived with nothing (worldly) and died with even less. Do you see the shift? We immediately evaluate and measure Jesus' life from a kingdom perspective rather than a worldly one. If we find our abundant life in our relationship with him, shouldn't we apply the same perspective to our lives?

That may feel like a stretch. After all, Jesus is God. He's part of the Trinity, who came from heaven and has returned to be seated at the right hand of God the Father. Of course we view his life differently. So let's look instead at the people around him. They not only personally heard him declare he is the Good Shepherd; they experienced it. They also heard him say he came to give them abundant life, yet the New Testament both depicts and predicts persecution for the early church. Extrabiblical accounts detail that nearly all of Jesus' disciples (and many other followers) were not only persecuted but also martyred.

I don't presume our lives to be the same, or even similar, to that of Jesus or the disciples. However, their lives lend a healthy perspective to this important truth: the Lord's gift of his presence brings abundant life, and this is a far more profound reality than financial comfort. The life we have through our Lord's shepherding presence is abundantly valuable and precious and eternally significant.

The Error that Money is Evil

"The love of money is a root of all kinds of evil" (1 Timothy 6:10). We are taught that money

leads to inevitable corruption, greed, and selfishness. Poverty is next to godliness. We must not have; and what we do have, we must give away.

First, let's look at this particular Scripture and then at the broader misunderstanding. The apostle Paul stated in his letter to Timothy that the love of money is a root of all kinds of evil. Other versions arguably translate the sentence more emphatically as the love of money *is* the root of all evil. It would be wrong to dismiss this serious caution. Whether the love of money is *a* root of evil, *the* root of *all* evil, or even if this phrase is hyperbole (an exaggeration to make the point more strongly), it is a warning everyone should take seriously. There is a strong, even direct, connection between the love of money (the root) and evil (the fruit).

However, notice specifically that the issue is the *love* of money, not money itself. Paul warned his young protégé, Timothy, about a heart issue or spiritual issue, not a matter of possessions. Paul made this clear distinction throughout his entire discussion. In the preceding verse, he stated that those who long to, or desire to, get rich are at risk of temptations and traps because of that pursuit. In the subsequent verse, in contrast to the pursuit of money, Paul charged Timothy to pursue righteousness, godliness, faith, love, endurance, and gentleness.

Then, without any critique or value placed on having money or not having money, Paul concluded his teaching in verses 17-19 with instruction for those who were *"rich in this present world."* He told Timothy to command them not to be arrogant or proud and to make sure they didn't put their hope in their wealth but rather placed their hope squarely in God and his riches. The rich were to find their enjoyment in those godly riches; they were to do good by being *"rich in good deeds,"* and being *"generous"* and *"willing to share."* These are the true treasures that form the firm foundation on which they could build their lives.

This distinction between the love of money and money itself may seem minor, but it is significant. Money is a possession. The love of money is a spiritual matter. Having money describes a state of affairs. The love of money describes a heart's desire that consumes our attention, alters our priorities, and even contends for our worship. As Paul stated here, the love of money shifts our hope away from God and to our own provision.

When our perspective on money is flawed, other truths get intertwined, distorting our view of the grace of giving and receiving and of poverty and prosperity and the spiritual dynamics associated with them. We already have examined these topics, but here we are simply clarifying the distinction between money and the love of money. Although money provides many opportunities for pitfalls, the Bible does not say money is evil. Rather, the Bible makes clear that a heart attitude that places love and hope in money is a root that will produce evil.

The Error That Duty Requires Us to Give

"The Scripture says, 'Do not muzzle the ox while it is treading out the grain,' and 'The worker deserves his wages'" (1 Timothy 5:18). We are taught that we have an obligation to give to the church. We have an obligation to keep the church doors open, and if they close, we are to blame.

The problem with this false pillar of kingdom financial perspective is its heart, or intent. It is less a matter of misunderstanding Scripture than of misapplying it. There should be a life-giving dimension in the joyful act of worship through giving. Instead, the spiritual act of giving is used as leverage to fulfill the financial needs of the local church. Bills need to be paid. Salaries need to be met. Ministries desire growth. Some churches are just trying to keep their doors open. In desperation, they take a holy act of worship and sacrificial giving and turn it into the duty of a good Christian. Some even go as far as assessing people's commitment to the Lord by measuring their giving to the local church.

This is an uncomfortable misunderstanding to articulate, but it is very widespread and deeply rooted in many church cultures. It also fuels a prevalent contention so many have with the church; namely, that the church only wants their money. This creates a formidable barrier between God's love and his children. We need to break down this issue.

Giving Is a Spiritual Act of Worship. From Genesis to Revelation, Scripture calls us to have a heart of giving and to practice giving. God is a generous God. We are made in his image, and therefore we are to be generous people. Jesus said freely you have received, so freely give (Matthew 10:8). Jesus said to give to the Lord that which is the Lord's (Matthew 22:21). And in the verse above, Paul quoted Jesus as saying that a worker of the gospel is worthy of his wages (see Luke 10:7). The error is not found in giving. The error comes when the motivation dismisses the spiritual significance. Giving is a spiritual act of worship. Second Corinthians describes it as the grace of giving, listing it along with faith and love (8:7). Giving rightly flows from a joyful relationship with the heavenly Father. One of the fastest ways to limit the flow of that provision is with a wrong heart attitude.

God desires that we always operate from the "inside out." Inside is our heart, our spirit; outside are our actions, words, and even decisions. When we operate from the "inside out," our outside actions are motived by the heart inside us, which reflects his love and life. However, if we invert our thinking and operate from the "outside in," we are viewing, managing, controlling, and even trying to manipulate our relationship with our heavenly Father. We want our actions to merit his approval, yet we actually distance ourselves from the blessings that otherwise flow so freely.

Relying on Our Own Strengths and Resources. We further exacerbate the situation by relying on our own strengths and resources and then layering our efforts with spiritual language to obligate others. We say, "God will provide," and then we try to meet the need from our own pockets. For example, leaders of a ministry may say they are confident the Lord has called them to venture into a new arena, but in order for this new ministry initiative to blossom, it will require everyone's dutifully given contribution. In essence, what is being said is, "We must fund God's calling." And we wonder why the promises of the Lord and the provision of the Lord seem so distant?

Acts 4 concludes with a description of some of the dynamics of the burgeoning church in its very first days of existence. Newcomers were joining the movement in droves. They were so captivated and transformed by the power and grace they were experiencing, they made radical commitments to the Lord and to each other. The entire Acts 4 narrative speaks to this commitment and empowering zeal and especially their wholehearted commitment to care for one another.

All the believers were one in heart and mind. No one claimed that any of his possessions was his own, but they shared everything they had. ... There were no needy persons among them. For from time to time those who owned lands or houses sold them, brought the money from the sales and put it at the apostles' feet, and it was distributed to anyone as he had need. (Act 4:32-35)

What a great testimony this was to the power and love that launched the church. As believers we should be inspired and challenged by such a captivating heritage. Yet, we must not be inspired and challenged simply by the actions but by the heart attitude that existed in this commonwealth perspective. The early believers' hearts were transformed to be like Christ, who considered others before himself. That's what's powerful and inspirational; that's what's captivating. Here was a community so committed to the reality of the presence of God's kingdom — and to each other — that they lived in profound devotion to God and one another. What a great expression this was of "inside out" living. The heart within motived the radical actions.

The easy mistake would be to try to replicate such a community or such actions through mandating that people give what they have for the common good ("outside in"). This wonderful picture of "inside out" love and devotion can't be duplicated by demanding that those who have give to those who have not. We shouldn't reverse the window into the early church that portrays a beautiful picture and turn it into a command to do likewise. The incredible outcome in the early church was the result of a heart attitude, not a command. It was not a duty or an obligation. The story told in Acts is descriptive, not prescriptive. The difference is subtle but most significant.

Notice that the passage says *"from time to time"* those who had possessions were liquidating them so they could share with others. The New International Version is the only translation to use the phrase *"time to time,"* but its intent is found in most translations. Instead of saying that all the believers "sold" what they had and brought the proceeds to the apostles, most translations state that believers "were selling" or "would sell" their possessions. It happened freely and often, but this is an observation, not a command. The early believers desired to help others. They gave from their heart's desire, not from any obligation placed upon them by the apostles.

Again, this is a subtle but significant difference that can best be clarified by considering the different emotions that arise from heart-motivated giving and obligatory giving. Let's envision ourselves in the Acts 4 community. If we are obligated to sell our personal possessions and share them with the community, we are dutifully bound to obey. Do you feel the weight of obligation and responsibility? Does that feel like freedom? However, if instead we are devoted to one another and a common goal and there exists such a real presence of the love and life of God that generosity and compassion do not need to be conscripted but naturally overflow to one another, then we are wholeheartedly bound to action but are driven by love. Does that warm your heart? Do you feel the joy of giving and blessing others? The end result in both approaches may look the same from the outside, but it couldn't be more different to those who are experiencing it.

Acts illustrates the difference between heart-motivated giving and obligatory giving in the next two stories. First, we read about Joseph.

> *Joseph, a Levite from Cyprus, whom the apostles called Barnabas (which means Son of Encouragement), sold a field he owned and brought the money and put it at the apostles' feet.* (Acts 4:36-37)

The author illustrated what he had just described about the early church community with a specific example. Joseph, a man who was such an encourager that they actually nicknamed him Barnabus (Son of Encouragement), sold a field so the money from the sale could be shared with those who needed it.

The contrast is illustrated by the next story. There is an unfortunate chapter break that tends to separate these two stories. However, they are intended as a pair, for they both relate to the community environment that is being described. Joseph the encourager exemplified that environment.

Acts 5 begins with the story of Ananias and his wife Sapphira, who also sold a piece of property. They took only some of the money from this transaction and gave it to the apostles so that it also could be shared with those in need. That sounds great, and it would have been great and even blessed if they had been honest about what they had done. Instead, they wanted people to believe they gave the full amount of the sale to the apostles, not a partial amount. They sought recognition for their actions but were not truthful about those actions. They alleged they were operating from a generous heart and God's love, when in fact their self-serving desire to be recognized stained their heart attitude. In this community of deep love, Ananias and Sapphira attempted to buy favor. What's worse, they were buying it with money they stole from the Lord. When the apostles confronted them with their lie, they were both instantly struck dead. Rather than giving as an expression of God's kingdom and his love for others, they sought to elevate themselves in the process. In their attempt to steal some of God's glory, they touched what was holy and bore the ultimate consequence.

Peter's commentary throughout the story makes it clear. The property was theirs, and they had no obligation to sell. Even when they did sell, the issue was not whether they gave the full or a partial amount to the apostles. The offense was that they lied, claiming to be giving the entire amount when in fact they were holding back a portion for themselves. They were attempting to fool the apostles and, the Scriptures say, even the Holy Spirit.

Giving is an act of worship. When we give to the Lord or to his kingdom purposes, we worship him. Done with a heart attitude of love and devotion to God, compassion and generosity to others, and selfless intent, it is a worshipful fragrance before the Lord. It glorifies God. When we reduce giving to a duty, we rob God of glory. When we give with the wrong motive, it doesn't bring glory to God. It isn't blessed. It doesn't fuel God's dynamic expression of overflowing love or kingdom presence (like in Acts 4). It is no longer a spiritual act of worship.

Duty and obligation can be antithetical to the very act of giving. Obligatory giving stifles the very purpose of giving. Measuring, controlling, manipulating, and requiring giving is an "outside in" mistake. Wholehearted generosity that flows out of a love relationship with our heavenly Father is an "inside out," life-giving flow.

These three false pillars of God's economy (the prosperity gospel, viewing money as evil, and giving solely out of duty) undermine the glorious and life-giving dimension of God's kingdom. They rob us of joy and partnership with God and his kingdom purposes. They are counterproductive to the witness of God's provision to us and to our witness to the world.

God is a generous God, a bountiful God, a God who delights in blessing us. It is for freedom that Christ sets us free. Let's build our understanding on God's truths, for they will bring us out of bondage to the world's economy and into the freedom of the kingdom's economy. To do that, we must be kingdom economists, renew our perspective, and avoid the snares of false teachings. We must embrace the life-giving flow of God's economy. "May your kingdom come…" includes the freedom of that great kingdom.

Removing Offense

In addition to strongholds erected from false teaching, there is also another very real snare that hides just below the surface, waiting to trip us up. We may actually struggle with God's kingdom economy because we are carrying the baggage of *offense*. Just think of all the places and ways we can cloud our perspective because of an underlying offense.

We may take offense at the very thought that God would ask for some of our money. We may take offense at demanding and controlling pastors and sermons about giving. We may be offended at God for not responding to our faithful giving and meeting our needs. We may be offended at churches that seem only to want our money. We may be offended at the responsibility heaped on us by others that we must give to keep the doors of the church open. Need I go on?

These offenses, this baggage, can at least color, if not greatly interfere with, our ability to learn any truth and gain any understanding about God's economy. If we attempt to view God's kingdom economy through the filter of our offenses, we'll blur our vision, and we won't gain the full, clear understanding that leads to freedom. Giving, generosity, gratitude, and the other principles we've addressed are spiritual matters. In order to fully understand and receive God's desire for blessings to flow to us, we must approach the topic of finances with the right attitude and perspective. Psalm 24 states that we are to approach the dwelling place of the Lord (which includes understanding his righteousness) with clean hands and a pure heart. We do not want to limit what the Lord would have for us because we are unwilling to let go of offenses.

As a pastor and church leader, I am aware of the manipulation, control, and self-serving counter purposes that have all too often found their way into teachings about giving and finances. I also recognize the self-serving nature of many financial appeals by either the church or Christian leaders. The purpose of the church should be to equip and release believers to be mature citizens of God's kingdom so that they may present God and his kingdom to the world around them. The purpose of the church should never be to sustain itself. Our desire should be for the kingdom to thrive, not for the church to survive. The details of any specific offense in this area may be something you may need to address further, but for now I ask you to please receive my apology as a pastor and on behalf of the church.

There is also another side to this same coin called offense, and that is that our own trust issues and need to control can cloud our perspective and misshape our judgment. When we reject the truth in Scripture and genuinely sound teaching, we judge, take offense, and give ourselves permission to dismiss principles that God intends for blessing. I encourage all of us to acknowledge our part in being offended, sometimes even giving ourselves permission to dismiss the topic of finances and giving altogether. Let's lay down the baggage of offense, even if some of it is well founded. Forgiveness frees us from the weight of the offense so that we may open ourselves fully to freedom in Christ in all areas of our lives, including our finances.

My hope is that now, after examining all we have covered, we might revisit any lingering offenses with a clearer understanding and be able to face them in an appropriate way. There may be particular situations to address. There may be situations or attitudes we can dismiss. There may be some areas where new clarity will lead to a healthier perspective, not only in what we think but also in our heart's attitude toward God, the church, and others. Let's give ourselves the best chance for truth and understanding to prevail. Let's open ourselves to the Father's heart, and let's trust in his goodness. May we truly be *"transformed by the renewing of [our] mind"* (Romans 12:2). Let's seek and expect to find the financial freedom for which Christ set us free. Let's look at God's economy without lenses of offense but through clean lenses and become kingdom economists!

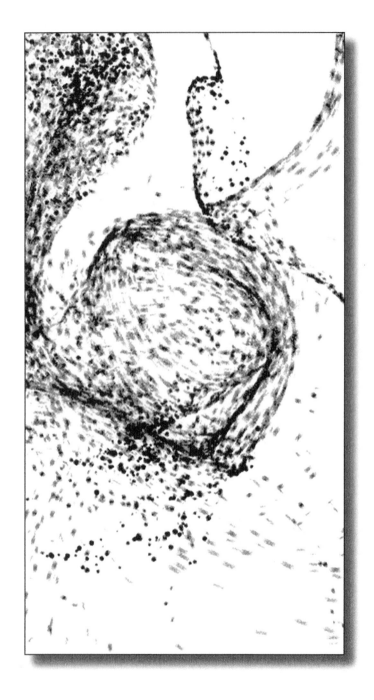

God's Kingdom Economy

*One person gives freely, yet gains even more;
another withholds unduly, but comes to poverty.
A generous person will prosper; whoever refreshes
others will be refreshed.* (Proverbs 11:24-25)

Givers and Takers

Picture yourself sitting in a room full of friends. The conversation banters back and forth, and although quite meaningless, it engages everyone's attention. The talkers talk, and the listeners listen, while everyone breathes in the warm atmosphere that quickly permeates the room, creating a subconscious but deeply perceived comfortable welcome to all. Everyone is refreshed simply by being in the company of friends.

Then in walks Taker. Taker needs something. Taker always needs something. This isn't because of his circumstances but rather regardless of his circumstances. Taker never seems content. Taker always has a problem or a situation, complete with its weighty burden. Or Taker has a need that to him is all-consuming, at least for the moment. Even when things are going well for Taker, there still is some situation or interaction or relationship that consumes his attention and drains his energy. Many people experience more than their share of difficulties in life. However, Taker is unable to face the difficulties or circumstances with perspective. Instead, the circumstances always dominate his perspective, his thoughts, and as a result his conversation and demeanor. Unable or unwilling to carry the burden or deal with the difficulty in healthy and helpful ways, Taker continually imposes his situation upon everyone. An unstoppable, cold draft invades the previously warm atmosphere.

When Taker enters the room, the casual conversation shifts to the weighty concern he imposes upon the group. I'm not labeling Taker as a bad person or necessarily manipulative. He is a friend, even someone who is valued and appreciated, but today's scene resembles an all-too-common and prevalent interaction with him. The group tries to attend to the situation. Some people respond with advice and counsel. Others share compassion and support through prayer and personal ministry to Taker. He thanks everyone, and yet even before leaving the room Taker resumes the posture of burden bearer (his own burdens, that is), as he picks back up the conversation and the weight he arrived with. Even worse, He has drained the rest of the group as well. Taker came in empty, Taker leaves empty, and Taker leaves everyone else feeling empty too.

Now, consider the same setting, but this time Giver enters the room. We all know Giver. She seems to live above the circumstances and situations that weave in and out of her life. Even when her circumstances are difficult, she's not carrying a heavy burden. Giver brings lightness, and it always spills over onto everyone she meets. She may not be the life of the party, but she is the light of the party. When she leaves, everyone feels uplifted and glad for the visit. Giver came in full, Giver leaves full, and Giver leaves others feeling full too.

Givers are never empty. Takers are never full. We've all experienced these two categories of people to some degree or other. There are givers, whom we look forward to being around because we will receive from their flow. And there are takers, and we know it is best to be prepared for an encounter with them because they will draw deeply from us. Why is this? Why do givers, who seem to give of themselves so naturally, always have an abundance of themselves to continually give away? Why is it that takers become empty faster than they can be filled and refilled?

The principles of God's economy are not limited to finances. They are evident in the full spectrum of our lives. Those who carry hope can freely pour out great measures of hope upon others, and yet they always have more to share. Faith-filled people shower faith upon everyone from a never-ending fountain of faith. Whether it's love, peace, confidence, joy, or any of the wellsprings of God's kingdom, the truth of opening channels for heaven's flow is witnessed before all of us if we have eyes to see. We can choose to be takers and keep for ourselves, or we can choose to be givers, blessing others with whatever we have, knowing our heavenly Father's sufficiency will never run out.

Living Water or Broken Cisterns

At one point when the Israelite nation had walked away from serving God, the Lord spoke this principle to them in a very direct way through the prophet Jeremiah. He said, *"My people have committed two sins: they have forsaken me, the spring of living water, and have dug their own cisterns, broken cisterns that cannot hold water"* (Jeremiah 2:13). The spring of living water is the never-ending flow of heaven's fullness. The cisterns are our attempts to meet our own needs and to be our own provider. The Lord considered the Israelites' actions to be sinful in two ways. Turning away from the spring of living water cut them off from the resources of heaven and the relationship with their heavenly Father. Building their own cisterns also grieved the Father because they were attempting to meet their own needs, which was something only he could truly do.

The cisterns are the world's economy. We feel we need to provide for ourselves, which means we need to do what we can and hold on to it as best we can. Yet, this verse reveals that our attempts to substitute our own solutions in place of God's provision will not work. Like cracked cisterns, our own solutions and efforts will leak. We will miss the spring of the life-giving flow, and we will toil to fill what will always fail. Givers have found the spring of living water. Giving with our finances is no different. There is a spring, a flow, available from our relationship and rightly postured heart with our heavenly Father.

Consider this proverb: *"One person gives freely, yet gains even more; another withholds unduly, but comes to poverty. A generous person will prosper; whoever refreshes others will be refreshed"* (Proverbs 11:24-25). Solomon's wisdom and observation is clear. Give, and you will gain more and even prosper. Withhold, and you enter the pathway toward poverty. Notice the two descriptions of the giving, generous person. The gifts are freely given, and they are for the refreshment (blessing) of others. This speaks of a spirit of generosity. It is not under compulsion or obligation. In fact, the phrase *"one person gives freely"* in the original Hebrew actually speaks of "one who scatters," and the phrase *"a generous person"* is literally a "soul of blessing." This person generously sows seed out of a desire to bless others. The parable is not simply about the act of giving but describes the heart's desire of the giver. This is the cheerful giver described in 2 Corinthians 9.

Also, notice the description of the one headed toward poverty. The Hebrew text here is literally "comes to lack." Someone who withholds unduly is responding to a spirit of poverty, which we defined as a fear of not having or a fear of losing. This is not withholding for good stewardship; it is withholding unduly. Instead of considering others' situations, such people are considering themselves first. However, by withholding unduly, they actually come to lack. They end up with the very thing their withholding is trying to prevent.

The results speak of givers and takers. Cheerful givers bless others with what they have. They don't worry about clinging to what they have out of a spirit of fear. As they position their hearts toward others, they also position themselves to receive more. As they bless others, they are blessed. They are sowing generously and therefore reaping generously. The harvest is more seed and righteousness. That means they have more seed to sow, and they receive a reward of righteousness from the Lord.

Those who sow sparingly withhold unduly. They do not sow more because their eyes are on themselves and they don't trust the Lord to provide all they need.

Givers enter a room, a situation, or a need and bless the situation from a heart of generosity. In the process they open a flow from heaven that allows them to receive even more, and they are refreshed as they refresh others. Takers enter a room, a situation, or a need with their attention squarely focused on themselves. Yet even while they withhold, or take more for themselves, they actually cut off the flow of available provision to themselves. They neither bless others nor gain anything for themselves. This concise two-sentence proverb contains many of the foundational principles found in God's kingdom economy: the principle of firstfruits, the understanding of flow, the grace of giving, a spirit of generosity, and the law of sowing and reaping.

Above anything else, we must recognize that the Lord is ultimately the source of all we have. We praise and honor him as our provider with a posture of firstfruits, and we give to the Lord our offering of worship and obedience. Our hope is to know him as our Jehovah-Jireh, "The Lord Our Provider." We humble ourselves and recognize his faithful Father's heart to provide all we need at all times for all things. Our hope is not in what we have or what we don't have. Our hope is in our God, who says, "I got this." We put our confidence in him, and we maintain our relationship as obedient worshippers.

The Miracle Wine

On the tiny island nation of Cyprus, there is a little-known community and otherwise insignificant four-acre parcel of land that experiences the truths and principles of God's kingdom economy. Gateways Beyond International is a community of believers committed to sharing a life of daily worship and prayer, discipleship training, and world outreach. Their commitment to this vision began in the late 1990s and continues today. After a number of years of concerted effort toward establishing their community and training school, Gateways Beyond felt prompted by the Lord to make an even deeper investment and commitment to the nation and land of Cyprus. They purchased a four-acre plot of land, complete with a small, neglected vineyard and a handful of olive trees scattered about. To their commitments to worship, prayer, training, and outreach, the community now added farming, although they were novices at best. With helpful advice and instruction from older Cypriots in the local village, they soon were harvesting grapes and olives and producing wine and olive oil. Then they added honeybees and sheep, and now they have a rather complete little operation on what they refer to as The Land.

However, the wonderfully inspiring part of their story is the profound blessing of the Lord that rests on everything that comes forth from The Land. From water for irrigation in an arid climate when the island was experiencing a seven-year drought to the quantity and quality of every harvest, this unassuming piece of earth operates in an economy distinctly different from the land around it. I'll share one story that parallels the Bible stories we've discussed throughout this book and epitomizes the favor resting on The Land and its caretakers.

In August 2011 after picking that year's small harvest of grapes, the group of believers began looking for a winery that would press them. This proved difficult since they were such a small operation. Expectations were low, and it was late in the season, which meant the sweetness of the grapes was questionable. In addition, the vineyard had not been treated to ward off flies or diseases. However, the winemaker who finally agreed to press their grapes was shocked at the amount of juice he easily squeezed out. Then, testing the quality, the winemaker called it miracle wine and the best Commandaria (a type of wine) in all of Cyprus. The winemaker even questioned the purity because wine of this quality and sweetness is achieved only by adding alcohol or other substitutes. The novice farmers found this laughable. In fact, they did not even understand what the winemaker was suggesting. "All we know how to do is pick grapes!" they said.

But the miracle was not over, for it was now time to transfer the wine to the oak barrel for aging. The wine already had been transferred between vats a number of times to remove sediment, so the exact quantity was well known. However, after they filled the oak barrel and the additional bottles and containers they knew they would need in order to hold all the wine, there was still more wine in the vat. They gathered more containers and asked neighbors for containers and filled every one of them. Not until they filled every last container they could find and then turned to a plastic kitchen bowl did the flow of wine finally end. The wine was already of higher quality than the professional winemakers knew how to create. Now there was a miraculous increase in the quantity as well!

This is not an ancient Bible story. This is today's world and today's kingdom economy. I've personally visited The Land in Cyprus. I've stood in the vineyard and the wine house. I've seen and touched that vat from which the wine flowed, and I've looked with anticipation at the oak barrel aging its contents. At the time of this writing, the aging process is just completing, and they are preparing to bottle the wine. You know my name is on the list to purchase some of the miracle wine!

Clearly the Lord has chosen to bless The Land, and it's appropriate to view this blessing in light of how the Gateways Beyond community lives out the principles we've discussed. I can attest firsthand to the generous lifestyle, the grace of giving, and the general understanding of God's kingdom economy that flows through their ministry. What we label as miraculous because it seems supernatural may simply be what is naturally found in God's kingdom economy. We can see the Lord's principles at work all around us if we choose to be kingdom economists.

We also should recognize the timing of this great testimony of God's favor upon the Gateways Beyond community and The Land. While they were experiencing God's economy alive, vibrant, and flowing around them, the country of Cyprus itself was in a downward spiral financially, heading toward complete failure. The Cypriot economy is overwhelmingly based on banking and the practices of getting all you can and taking advantage of everyone and every situation for your own gain. The seemingly glowing economy just a few years prior was actually a financial house of cards that collapsed upon itself. The European Union agreed to bail out the tiny island nation (at least initially), but it came at a painfully deep cost to the citizens of Cyprus.

Yet here in the midst of a failed worldly economic system thrives a wellspring of God's economy. In a country reeling from an economy that has dried up sits a community flowing with provision. The stark contrast is poignant. Let me also be very clear: the Gateways community is by no means overflowing in resources. They are living and operating their ministry on the thinnest of financial means. Money is not overflowing but scarce, yet without question abundant life flows. They experience all they need when they need it. They increasingly have more seed to sow (measured in more ways than money), and they most definitely are and will continue to reap a harvest of righteousness.

(Not only was I blessed to be able to visit the island of Cyprus and the Gateways Beyond community, but I also wrote a significant amount of this book during my extended stay there in their hospitality. This was not why I went to visit them, and they did not really know about or contribute to the book. However, the experience was quite captivating to me. The Lord has been inspiring and developing my understanding and experience of his kingdom and his economy my whole life. In his providence, I found myself inspired to finish writing this book while in the vortex of the collapsed Cypriot economy and in the harvest of God's economy being experienced by the Gateways community in the foothills of Cyprus. It was an inspiration, a privilege, and a blessing.)

God's Kingdom Economy

The flow we find in God's kingdom is in fact very natural. A stream that is dammed up becomes stagnant. Creatures inhabiting that stream will begin to die. Break open the dam and release the flow of water, and the stream becomes a source of life again. In the economy of God, we give away what we have, agreeing with our Lord's prayer that his kingdom will come and his will be done on this earth. But God's kingdom does not begin by measuring actions and deeds. It begins in the heart. As we align our hearts with the Lord's heart, we will desire to bless others and open channels of his grace. Flow is as natural with our resources as with any of God's glorious attributes. As we give, we open a flow of heaven's resources, which are completely sufficient.

Giving is actually a spiritual grace we can pursue. As we do so, we move from a mind-set of poverty and prosperity to an understanding of the spirit of poverty and the spirit of generosity. Joy rushes in when we flow and overflow with generosity, regardless of our own circumstances. Tremendous freedom comes when we leave the spirit of poverty behind and begin to experience the joy of serving and blessing others.

A lifestyle of generosity is available to all of us. Choosing to sow generously, knowing God will bring his abounding grace allows us to be free and cheerful as we give. We also position ourselves to become channels of generous seed that will multiply its fruitful blessing as it's sown into the world and into the lives of others. Through it all, God will be praised and receive the glory.

"It is for freedom that Christ has set us free. Stand firm, then, and do not let yourselves be burdened again by a yoke of slavery" (Galatians 5:1). Let's not remain enslaved in the snares of finances and the confusion surrounding gratitude, generosity, and giving. Even as we talk about money, we understand that it's not actually about the money. The principles of God's economy begin with the heart. Firstfruits and tithing reflect our posture before they are percentages. Gratitude is a heart declaration that recognizes God as our loving, caring Father who will provide all we need. We express our gratitude in our monetary offerings, but those offerings are expressions of our hearts. Generosity is a product of hearts that love our neighbors as ourselves. Generosity is not something to be measured but to be experienced, a lifestyle of living in the abounding grace of heaven's flow. Giving is an act of worship to the Lord, our Provider, and a sowing into his kingdom. Giving seeks to bless others, to reap a reward of righteousness,

and to bring glory to God. Gratitude, generosity, and giving are expressed through how we handle our money. However, freedom in finances is found when we don't manage our money in order to save or give but rather when our money is managed by hearts and minds operating in God's economy and its principles.

As we live in this world and as we live as citizens of God's kingdom, there is no static, fixed, and unchanging place of solitude where we can hide. We are either growing with God, or we are experiencing the pull of entropy from this world. We are either increasing and advancing with God's purposes for us and through us to the world, or we are fading in our significance and our ability to impact and influence the world and those around us. My desire is that the realm of finances would no longer be an area of struggle, striving, and frustration for believers and followers of Jehovah-Jireh. My desire is that we would experience the freedom for which Christ has set us free. My desire is for the body of Christ to be economists who understand, believe, and release the economy of God's kingdom. May his economy come, on earth as it is in heaven!

CPSIA information can be obtained at www.ICGtesting.com
Printed in the USA
BVOW11s1705260214

346085BV00005B/9/P